PENGUIN BOOKS

EIGHT CHAMBERS OF T

Marge Piercy was born in Detroit and grew up there. She now lives in Wellfleet on Cape Cod with her husband, the novelist and screenwriter Ira Wood, and has previously lived in Chicago, Boston, Paris, San Francisco and New York. Since the mid-sixties, she has been active in the women's movement but has also been involved with other political issues, notably civil rights, the New Left and the anti-nuclear movement. She lives by her writing and by giving poetry readings and workshops.

Marge Piercy has written many previous volumes of poetry including *Breaking Camp*, *Hard Loving*, *To Be of Use*, *Living in the Open*, *The Twelve-Spoked Wheel Flashing*, *The Moon is Always Female*, *Stone, Paper, Knife*, *My Mother's Body*, *Circles on the Water* (her selected poems), *Available Light* and *Mars and Her Children*. She is also the author of several bestselling novels, of which Penguin publishes *Braided Lives*, *Vida*, *Small Changes*, *Gone to Soldiers*, *Summer People*, *Body of Glass*, (winner of the 1993 Arthur C. Clarke Award) and *The Longings of Women*.

MARGE PIERCY

Eight Chambers of the Heart

PENGUIN BOOKS

PENGUIN BOOKS

Published by the Penguin Group
Penguin Books Ltd, 27 Wrights Lane, London w8 5tz, England
Penguin Books USA Inc., 375 Hudson Street, New York, New York 10014, USA
Penguin Books Australia Ltd, Ringwood, Victoria, Australia
Penguin Books Canada Ltd, 10 Alcorn Avenue, Toronto, Ontario, Canada m4v 3b2
Penguin Books (NZ) Ltd, 182–190 Wairau Road, Auckland 10, New Zealand

Penguin Books Ltd, Registered Offices: Harmondsworth, Middlesex, England

Published in Penguin Books 1995
10 9 8 7 6 5 4 3 2 1

Copyright © Middlemarsh, Inc., 1995
All rights reserved
The moral right of the author has been asserted

Set by Datix International Limited, Bungay, Suffolk
Printed in England by Clays Ltd, St Ives plc
Filmset in 10/13pt Monophoto Bembo

Copyrights in the original publication of the poems in this volume were
established in 1963, and in each year between 1968 and 1994 inclusive.

Except in the United States of America, this book is sold subject
to the condition that it shall not, by way of trade or otherwise, be lent,
re-sold, hired out, or otherwise circulated without the publisher's
prior consent in any form of binding or cover other than that in
which it is published and without a similar condition including this
condition being imposed on the subsequent purchaser

Contents

THE JUNGLE AND TUNDRA OF THE BED

HOUSE BUILT ON A SANDBAR

[viii]

Introduction

It is an odd situation to be introducing a survey of half my life's work so far to an audience almost entirely unfamiliar with it, many of whom have known me as a novelist but never before as a poet. In the States, I was published as a poet frequently and in a wide range of periodicals for several years before I ever had a story published; my first volume of poetry came out and my second was accepted before anyone would take a chance on a novel. I still give a great many readings in universities, libraries, theaters, community centers and at festivals – and it is almost always my poetry that audiences come to hear performed. In works from psychology texts to law reviews, it is the poems that are quoted.

Lines from my poetry are silkscreened on tee shirts, greeting cards and posters and woven into quilts, splashed over murals and painted on sheets to raise money or simply to give expression to something that people feel. Individual poems have been used in groups ranging from education classes for union members to recovery groups for rape victims or battered women. My liturgical poems are a frequent part of Jewish services. My poems are quoted by politicians and speakers at rallies. They have been used by choreographers in creating dances and as part of dramatic performances by amateur and professional groups. Poems have been included in two hundred anthologies. They are the sort of poems people sometimes carry in their wallets, put up on their refrigerators or over their computers. A number of people in the States feel that these poems belong to them in a personal, direct, emotional way.

I hope the poems can belong to you, the British reader, in the same way. Don't be too American, my British editor said, and left me stymied. I left out poems on the Vietnam war and on such American phenomena as the 4th of July and boom boxes. As I look at the poems, they are all quite American. However, like good rock music and rhythm and blues, they may have legs that can carry them into your culture. Perhaps you too may find poems that speak for you, even if they do it in a decidedly American accent.

My poems are meant to be read, recited, performed. On the page, they are notations about sounds and silences, waiting in those arrangements of black on white to be brought to life by your eyes and your voice. They want to be spoken conversationally, chanted, shouted. Some have been set to music.

An introduction might be a kind of envoi: Go little book out into the world and wheedle your way into the lives of strangers like a stray kitten. However, a Selected Poems is not little. Go fat book and impose upon strangers like a randy elephant, lacks appeal. I will settle for saying what I imagine I am doing.

I imagine that I speak for a constituency, living and dead, and that I give utterance to energy, experience, insight – words flowing from many lives. I have always desired my poems be meaningful for others. 'To be of use' is the title of one of my best-known poems. What I mean by *use* is not that the poems function as agitprop. I don't even mean didactic poetry, although I have no more hesitation than Pope or Hesiod did to work in that mode as well as others. The notion that poetry with a conscious rather than an unconscious politics is impermissible or impure is a modern heresy. We are social animals and we live with and off and on each other. You would have a great deal of trouble explaining to Sophocles, Virgil, Catullus, Chaucer, Dryden, Wordsworth, Shelley, Arnold, Whitman, Blake, Goethe, that poetry must refer only to other poetry and that poets are people who have no social connections, social interests, social duties.

What I mean by useful is simply that I hope readers will find poems that speak to and for them, will take those poems into their lives and say them to each other and remember bits and pieces of them in stressful or quiet moments. That the poems may give voice to something in the experience of a life has been my intent. To find ourselves spoken for in art gives dignity to our pain, our anger, our lust, our losses. We can hear what we hope for and what we fear in the small release of cadenced utterance. We have few rituals that function for us in the ordinary chaos of our severed lives.

I have not followed a chronological sequence in this volume, but rather have organized the poems around the areas of a woman's life and consciousness. Almost all the sections contain some poems written twenty-five years ago as well as some not yet collected in book form in the States. Probably the poems in some sections will mean more to you than those in others.

I have readers who love my poems about life near the ocean, about gardening, about zucchini (that rambunctious summer squash I think you call courgette?) and lettuce and tomatoes, and simply skip or tune out the poems about nuclear power or corporate greed. I have readers for whom the important poems are those about family or sexual relationships in all their glory and gore, and the others are just paper. Then there are readers who love the poems they call feminist or political, but ask why I waste time writing about herons or oak trees or cats.

I have to confess, to me it is all one vision. I have given the book the shape of a small world, the kitchen, the bedroom, the street, the workplace, the garden, the natural world. I have had twelve collections of poetry published so far, and to make this selection from them was difficult and a little frustrating. If my novels explore the roads I did not take but choose to travel and map imaginatively, the poems are far more that road I have taken. They are, for better and for worse, the fruit of my being. Computer freak and mystic, organizer and gardener, feminist and observant Jew and, for twelve years, a happily and passionately married woman, I come out of the stone-working class of Detroit, where class warfare and ethnic rage, racism, anti-Semitism, are all clear as billboards. I have been involved directly in civil rights, in the new left, in feminism. I have also followed my curiosity and my will for adventure and experience to some extremes and some disasters. I communicate well with cats and poorly with bureaucrats. If my life is sometimes contemplative now, it was anything but that for the first four decades, and all of the places I have lived and the many many people I have loved and fought with and against enter my work with their burdens and their energy.

It is of the nature of a highly selected volume like this one that few full sequences could be included. However, I included 'The Lunar Cycle', since it is so well known in the States. Another I have put in is called 'Underrated Pleasures'. I believe there are no poetic subjects, only subjects to which we pay the right kind of attention. This is a sequence about such mundane activities as folding bedsheets and planting bulbs. As the last poem in the volume says quite explicitly, I believe that love is a kind of attention we owe to the world, or at least that bit of it that we perceive.

IN THE SOUL'S KITCHEN

Putting the good things away

In the drawer were folded fine
batiste slips embroidered with scrolls
and posies, edged with handmade
lace too good for her to wear.

Daily she put on schmatehs
fit only to wash the car
or the windows, rags
that had never been pretty

even when new: somewhere
such dresses are sold only
to women without money to waste
on themselves, on pleasure,

to women who hate their bodies,
to women whose lives close on them.
Such dresses come bleached by tears,
packed in salt like herring.

Yet she put the good things away
for the good day that must surely
come, when promises would open
like tulips their satin cups

for her to drink the sweet
sacramental wine of fulfillment.
The story shone in her as through
tinted glass, how the mother

gave up and did without
and was in the end crowned
with what? scallions? crowned
queen of the dead place

in the heart where old dreams
whistle on bone flutes,
where run-over pets are forgotten,
where lost stockings go?

In the coffin she was beautiful
not because of the undertaker's
garish cosmetics but because
that face at eighty was still

her face at eighteen peering
over the drab long dress
of poverty, clutching a book.
Where did you read your dreams, Mother?

Because her expression softened
from the pucker of disappointment,
the grimace of swallowed rage,
she looked a white-haired girl.

The anger turned inward, the anger
turned inward, where
could it go except to make pain?
It flowed into me with her milk.

Her anger annealed me.
I was dipped into the cauldron
of boiling rage and rose
a warrior and a witch

but still vulnerable
there where she held me.
She could always wound me
for she knew the secret places.

She could always touch me
for she knew the pressure

points of pleasure and pain.
Our minds were woven together.

I gave her presents and she hid
them away, wrapped in plastic.
Too good, she said, too good.
I'm saving them. So after her death

I sort them, the ugly things
that were sufficient for every
day and the pretty things for which
no day of hers was ever good enough.

Hand games

Intent gets blocked by noise.
How often what we spoke
in the bathtub, weeping
water to water, what we framed
lying flat in bed to the spiked
night is not the letter we send.
We drive toward each other on express
ways without exits. The telephone
turns our voices into codes,
terms of an equation
that never balances, a scale
forever awry with its foot
stuck up lamely like a scream.

Drinking red wine from a sieve,
trying to catch love in words,
its strong brown river in flood

pours through our weak bones.
A kitten will chase the beam of a flash
light over the floor. We learn
some precious and powerful forces
can not be touched, and what
we touch plump and sweet
as a peach from the tree, a tomato
from the vine, sheds the name
as if we tried to write in pencil
on its warm and fragrant skin.

Mostly the television is on
and the washer is running and the kettle
shrieks it's boiling while the telephone
rings. Mostly we are worrying about
the fuel bill and how to pay the taxes
and whether the diet is working
when the moment of vulnerability
lights on the nose like a blue moth
and flitters away through clouds of mosquitoes
and the humid night. In the leaking
sieve of our bodies we carry
the blood of our love.

Eat fruit

Keep your legs crossed, Mother said. Drinking
leads to babies. Don't hang around street corners.
I rushed to gulp moonshine on corners, hip outthrust.
So why in the butter of my brain does one marble tablet
shine bearing my mother's commandment, eat fruit?

Here I stand, the only poet from whom
you can confidently obtain after a reading
enough mushy tan bananas to bake bread
should you happen to feel the urge at ten
some night in East Lansing or Boise.

You understand how needful it is, you say,
that I should carry the products of Cape
Cod such as oranges and kiwis with me
because surely they sell none in Seattle.
Suppose South America should be blockaded?

Others litter ash, beer cans. I leak pits.
As we descend into Halifax while my seat partner
is snorting the last of his coke, I am the one
choking as I gobble three apples in five minutes,
agricultural contraband seized at borders.

Customs agents throw open my suitcase and draw
out with gingerly leer from under my negligee
a melon. Drug smugglers feed their self-importance,
but me they hate along with the guy trying to smuggle
in a salami from the old country his uncle gave him.

I am the slob who makes gory stains on railroad seats
with fermenting strawberries. You can recognize me
by the happy cloud of winged creatures following my head.
I have raised more fruitflies than genetics labs.
I have endowed ant orphanages and retirement communities.

However, I tell you smugly, I am regular in Nome,
in Paducah, in both Portlands and all Springfields.
While you are eating McMuffins I am savoring a bruised
but extremely sophisticated pear that has seen five
airports and four cities and grown old in wisdom.

I have always been poor at flirting

I know it's harmless. My friends who flirt
the hardest – consummate, compulsive – are least
apt to fall into bed on a hot night's wind.
Flirting is what they do instead of sex,
five-year affairs of eyes and telephone trysts,
voices soft as warm taffy, artful laughs,
a hush when the spouse walks through the room.

Yet when I flirt I feel like an elephant
in a pink tutu balancing on a beach ball,
a tabby wearing a doll's dress, stuffed
in a carriage, about to snarl and slash.
I am pretending to be a girl, a girly girl.
A smile hangs on my face like a loose shutter.
My voice is petroleum jelly on my tongue.

My mother flirted with the milkman, the iceman,
the butcher – oh he winked and strutted,
flashing his gold tooth and slapping the scale.
Ogling, the plumber fixed both leaks
for the price of one. She flirted with the mailman,
the paperboy who brought our paper and only ours
to the door. I'd watch sour as a rotten lemon,

dour as a grandfather clock, cringing, muttering
Mother! like the curse word it was. The walls
would drip perfumed oil. The ceiling sagged buttery.
Her eyes were screwed wide open, Betty Boop,
batting butterfly wings, her mouth pursed,
while she played them like saxophones,
her voice now a tiny plush mouse,

now sleeking into the lower registers
of dark honey lapping at the belly.

[8]

When we couldn't pay the mortgage, she almost
climbed into the bank manager's lap.
Motorcycle cops pulling over our sputtering car,
teachers, principals, my father's bosses,
she had only one weapon, shameless silent

promises redeemable for absolutely nothing
but an ego job on the spot, frothing over.
If afterward she called them behayma,
fool, it was with quiet satisfaction,
an athlete who has performed well and won.
I remember the puzzled damaged look in her
widened eyes when flirting began to fail.

For some it is a drug of choice,
a moment's cocaine spiking the ego, giving
that spurt of a mirror cooing attraction.
For me it means only, I am powerless,
you can hurt or help me, wedged there above,
so I attempt this awkward dance of the broken
fan and the mud colored bubble, among your teeth.

Attraction to me is a walking toward,
the doors in the hands and the mind slowly
swinging on their hinges so that something
can pass over and something new enter.
This flicking of the body like a cape before
a bull, this mincing of the hook under the
feathers is more war and less love than I need.

Hello up there

Are you You or Me or It?
I go littering you over the furniture
and picking you out of the stew.
Often I've wished you otherwise: sleek,
docile, decorative and inert.
Yet even in daydreams I cannot imagine myself
otherwise thatched: coarse, black and abundant
like weeds burst from the slagheaps of abandoned mines.

In the 50s children used to point and shout Witch.
Later they learned to say Beatnik and later yet, Hippie,
but old grandmamas with Thessaloniki or Kiev in their throats
thought I must be nice because I looked like a peasant.
In college my mother tried to change my life
by bribing me to cut it off and have it 'done'.
Afterwards the hairdresser chased me waving my hair in a paper
    bag.
The next man who happened was a doctor's son
who quoted the Lord Freud in bed and on the pot,
thought I wrote poems because I lacked a penis
and beat me when he felt ugly.
I grew my hair back just as quick as I could.

Cloud of animal vibrations,
tangle of hides and dark places
you keep off the tidy and the overly clean and the wango
    upright.
You proclaim the sharp limits of my patience
with trying to look like somebody's wet dream.
Though I can trim you and throw you out with the coffee
    grounds,
when I am dead and beginning to smell worse than my shoes

presumably you will continue out of my skull
as if there were inside no brains at all
but only a huge bobbin of black wire unwinding.

Belly good

A heap of wheat, says the Song of Songs
but I've never seen wheat in a pile.
Apples, potatoes, cabbages, carrots
make lumpy stacks, but you are sleek
as a seal hauled out in the winter sun.

I can see you as a great goose egg
or a single juicy and fully ripe peach.
You swell like a natural grassy hill.
You are symmetrical as a Hopewell mound,
with the eye of the navel wide open,

the eye of my apple, the pear's port
window. You're not supposed to exist
at all this decade. You're to be flat
as a kitchen table, so children with
roller skates can speed over you

like those sidewalks of my childhood
that each gave a different roar under
my wheels. You're required to show
muscle striations like the ocean
sand at ebb tide, but brick hard.

Clothing is not designed for women
of whose warm and flagrant bodies
you are a swelling part. Yet I confess

I meditate with my hands folded on you,
a maternal cushion radiating comfort.

Even when I have been at my thinnest,
you have never abandoned me but curled
round as a sleeping cat under my skirt.
When I spread out, so do you. You like
to eat, drink and bang on another belly.

In anxiety I clutch you with nervous fingers
as if you were a purse full of calm.
In my grandmother standing in the fierce sun
I see your cauldron that held eleven children
shaped under the tent of her summer dress.

I see you in my mother at thirty
in her flapper gear, skinny legs
and then you knocking on the tight dress.
We hand you down like a prize feather quilt.
You are our female shame and sunburst strength.

The hunger moon

The snow is frozen moonlight on the marshes.
How bright it is tonight, the air thin
as a skim of black ice and serrated,
cutting the lungs. My eyes sting.

Spring, I watch the moon for instruction
in planting; summer, I gauge her grasp
on the tides of the sea, the bay, my womb:
now you may gather oysters, now lay

the white, the red, the black beans
into the earth eyes rolled upwards.
But winters, we are in opposition.
I must fight the strong pulls of the body.

The blood croons, curl to sleep, embryo in a seed.
Early to sleep, late to rise from the down cave.
Even at seven night squats in the pines.
Swim in the womb of dreams and grow new limbs.

Awake at last, the body begins to crave,
not salads, not crisp apples and sweet kiwis,
but haunches of beef and thick fatty stews.
Eat, whispers the crone in the bone, eat.

The hunger moon is grinning like a skull.
The bats are asleep. The little voles
streak starving through tunnels in the snow
and voracious shrews race after them.

Eat, make fat against famine, grow round
while there's something rich to gnaw on,
urges the crone from her peasant wisdom.
She wants every woman her own pumpkins,

she wants me full as tonight's moon
when I long to wane. Why must I fight her,
who taught my mother's mother's mothers
to survive the death marches of winters past?

The flying Jew

I never met my Uncle Dave.
The most real thing I know about him
is how he died, which he did
again and again in the middle of the night
my mother screaming, my father shouting,
Shut up, Bert, you're having a bad dream.

My Uncle Dave, the recurring nightmare.
He was the Jew who flew.
How did he manage it? Flying was for
gentlemen, and he was a kid from the slums
of Philadelphia, Pittsburgh, Cleveland –
zaydeh one headlong leap ahead of the law
and the Pinkertons, the goons who finally
bashed his head in when he was organizing
his last union, the bakery workers.

Dave looked up between the buildings,
higher than the filthy sparrows who pecked
at horse dung and the pigeons who strutted
and cooed in the tenement eaves,
up to the grey clouds of Philadelphia,
the rust clouds of Pittsburgh with the fires
of the open hearth steel mills staining them,
a pillar of smoke by day and fire by night.

He followed into the clouds.
My mother doesn't even know who taught
him to fly, but he learned.
He became one with the plane, they said.
Off he went to France. He flew in combat,
was shot down and survived, never

became an ace, didn't enjoy combat,
the killing, but flying was better than sex.

He took my mother up once and she wept
the whole time. She wouldn't fly again
till she was seventy-five and said then
she didn't care if the plane went down.

It was his only talent, his only passion
and a good plane was a perfect fit for
his body and his mind, his reflexes.
The earth was something that clung to his shoes,
something to shake off, something to gather
all your strength into a taut charge
and then launch forward and leave behind.

After the war, he was lost for two years,
tried selling, tried insurance, then off
he went barnstorming with his war buddies.
Time on the ground was just stalling time,
killing time, parked in roominghouses
and tourist homes and bedbug hotels.
He drank little. Women were aspirin.

Being the only Jew, he had something
to prove every day, so he flew the fastest,
he did the final trick that made the audience
shriek. The planes grew older, the crowds
thinned out. One fall day outside Cleveland
he got his mother, sister Bert and her
little boy to watch the act. It was a triple
Zimmerman roll he had done five hundred
shows but this time the plane plowed
into the earth and a fireball rose.

So every six months he died flaming
in the middle of the night, and all I
ever knew of him was Mother screaming.

Cats like angels

Cats like angels are supposed to be thin;
pigs like cherubs are supposed to be fat.
People are mostly in between, a knob
of bones sticking out in the knee you might
like to pad, a dollop of flab hanging
over the belt. You punish yourself,
one of those rubber balls kids have
that come bouncing back off their own
paddles, rebounding on the same slab.
You want to be slender and seamless
as a bolt.

      When I was a girl
I loved spiny men with ascetic grimaces
all elbows and words and cartilage
ribbed like cast up fog-grey hulls,
faces to cut the eyes blind
on the glittering blade, chins
of Aegean prows bent on piracy.

Now I look for men whose easy bellies
show a love for the flesh and the table,
men who will come in the kitchen
and sit, who don't think peeling potatoes
makes their penis shrink; men with broad
fingers and purple figgy balls,
men with rumpled furrows and the slightly
messed look at ease of beds recently
well used.

      We are not all supposed
to look like undernourished fourteen-year-
old boys, no matter what the fashions
ordain. You are built to pull a cart,

to lift a heavy load and bear it,
to haul up the long slope, and so
am I, peasant bodies, earthy, solid
shapely dark glazed clay pots that can
stand on the fire. When we put our
bellies together we do not clatter
but bounce on the good upholstery.

Beauty I would suffer for

Last week a doctor told me
anemic after an operation
to eat: ordered to indulgence,
given a papal dispensation to run
amok in delis.
Yet I know that in
two weeks, a month I
will have in my nostrils
not the savor of roasting goose,
not the burnt sugar of caramel topping
the Saint-Honoré cake, not the pumpernickel
bearing up the sweet butter, the sturgeon
but again the scorched wire,
burnt rubber smell
of willpower, living
with the brakes on.

I want to pass into the boudoirs
of Rubens' women. I want to dance
graceful in my tonnage like Poussin nymphs.
Those melon bellies, those vast ripening thighs,

those featherbeds of forearms, those buttocks
placid and gross as hippopotami:
how I would bend myself
to that standard of beauty, how faithfully
I would consume waffles and sausage for breakfast
with croissants on the side, how dutifully
I would eat for supper the blackbean soup
with Madeira, followed by the fish course,
the meat course, and the Bavarian cream.
Even at intervals during the day I would
suffer an occasional éclair
for the sake of appearance.

Unbuttoning

The buttons lie jumbled in a tin
that once held good lapsang souchong
tea from China, smoky as the smell
from a wood stove in the country,
leaves opening to flavor and fate.

As I turn buttons over, they sound
like strange money being counted
toward a purchase as I point
dumbly in a foreign bazaar,
coins pittering from my hand.

Buttons are told with the fingers
like worry beads as I search
the trove for something small
and red to fill the missing
slot on a blouse placket.

I carried them from my mother's
sewing table, a wise legacy
not only practical but better
able than fading snapshots
to conjure buried seasons.

Button stamped with an anchor
means my late grade-school pea coat.
Button in the form of a white
daisy from a sky blue dress
she wore, splashed with that flower,

rouses her face like a rosy dahlia
bent over me petaled with curls.
O sunflower hungry for joy
who turned her face through the years
bleak, withered, still yearning.

The tea was a present I brought
her from New York where she
had never gone and never would.
This mauve nub's from a dress
once drenched in her blood;

this, from a coral dress she wore
the day she taught me that word,
summer '41, in Florida:
'Watch the clipper ships take off
for Europe. Soon war will come to us.

'They will not rise so peacefully
for years. Over there they're
killing us and nobody cares.
Remember always. Coral is built
of bodies of the dead piled up.'

Buttons are useful little monuments.
They fasten and keep decently

shut and warm. They also open.
Rattling in my hand, they're shells
left by vanished flesh.

The price begins to mount

What gets you in its teeth in middle age
is not what we had imagined. Sex is perhaps
easier, less fraught, less imagined,
common and rich and something the body
has learned to do with another like tennis
but deeper and longer in its mind body meld.

Years ago in Denmark I struck my left elbow.
Some mornings it suddenly sings of rain and morbidity.
The Nazis who kneecapped me in Central Park under
the Viet Cong flag come back to me in their ferocity
when one bright morning translucent as a light gel
it gives under me, the ground rising to strike me.

It is the dizziness that presses with a heavy hand
on my head, bowing me toward my soft belly.
It is the organs you never knew you had singing out,
a liver, a gall bladder, adrenals, one evening
knocking you down the steps or turning your blood
to a viscid grey liquid that coats the eyes blind.

It is the moment that bad genes combine and come
on line, Hi there, this is Grandma's cancer reporting
from your stomach, the glaucoma of the father
who scarcely remembered your name stealing
your vision like a sneak, filing your optic nerve
to fraying while you sleep.

Half the population reads astrology columns
in the paper, the TV guide, yet we ignore
what is encoded in the genes tucked into each cell
tinier than the writing in mezuzahs.
Always we are shocked when a new trouble
Aunt Harriet had when we were seven kicks in.

Maybe your mother left you a jade necklace,
her ring, but this is the true inheritance,
cataracts dimming your vision and the tendency
to have your brain crack open with a stroke.
This is the real will your father produced,
that time bomb ticking in your chest like a heart.

A key to common lethal fungi

What rots it is taking
for granted. To assume what
is given you is laid on like the water
that rushes from the faucet singing
when you turn the tap. Wait
till the reservoir goes dry
to learn how precious are those
clear diamond drops.

We hunt our lovers like deer
through the thorny thickets and after
we have caught love we start
eating it to the bone.
We use it up in hamburgers
complaining of monotony.

We walk all over the common miracles
without bothering to wipe our feet.

Then we wonder why we need more
and more salt to taste our food.

My old man, my old lady, my
ball and chain: listen, even the cat
you found starving in the alley
who purrs you to sleep dancing
with kneading paws in your hair
will vanish if your heart closes its fist.

Habit's fine dust chokes us.
As in a city the streetlights
and neon signs prevent us from viewing
the stars, so the casual noise, the smoke
of ego turning over its engine blinds
us till we can no longer see past
our minor needs to the major constellations
of the ram, the hunter, the swan
that guide our finite gaze
through the infinite dark.

Litter

I am always forgetting something.
The kettle boils dry and stinks.
The tiny green-shouldered tomato plants
while I'm writing a poem die of thirst
scorched under the glass of the hotbed.

I forget birthdays, I forget to call.
I forget the book I promised to bring.
I forget where I put my purse, my keys,

my wallet, my lenses, my love.
I lose my way in night's black pocket.

I can't think of the name of the goddess
who stands at the gate blinking her one
great eye through the fog and the snarling
wind, sweeping her warning glance across
where the waves smash themselves kneeling.

I forget the way my mother laughed.
I forget her cake, the taste of the uncooked
dough, the just proportions of cinnamon and sugar.
I lose the touch of her fingers, stone
washed smooth by water and laid in the sun.

I lose the bread smell of my old cat's fur;
I lose the name and face of a man just out
of prison who crawled in my body to hide;
I lose the addresses of urgent people to whom
I promised much in towns I have forgotten.

What happened to my burnt orange shawl?
My bones are slowly dissolving in salt water.
It all falls away like feathers, like leaves,
like sand blowing. In the end I will say,
I was somebody maybe a woman I forget.

All the lost words and things and tasks
I have littered behind me are drifting on winds
round and up as if gravity had forgotten
to drop them, and sometimes in the night
I wake and the name comes to me and I shout

to the ceiling, Appomattox, rue de Sentier,
Emily Hannah, 8325 American Avenue,
metasomatism, two thirds to one,
and then lilacs, the scent of my mother's
white lilacs, thickens the air till I weep.

Does the light fail us, or do we fail the light?

1.
My old cat lives under a chair.
Her long fur conceals the sharp
jut of her fleshless bones.

Her eyes are dimmed by clouds
of cataract, only visible
if you remember their willow green

as I could judge my mother's
by calling up that fierce charred
brown gaze, smiting, searching.

When one of the young cats approaches
she growls in anger harmless
as distant thunder. They steal her food.

They do not act from malice.
They would curl up with her and wash.
She hisses fear. Her lifelong

companion died. They appeared.
Surely the young bear the blame
for all the changes that menace

in the fog of grey shapes looming.
Her senses that like new snow
had registered the brush strokes

of tracks, the fall of a pine needle,
the alighting of a chickadee;
her senses that had opened

greedy as the uncurling petals
of a sea anemone that drinks
the world's news from the current;

that tantalized her with message
of vole and shrew and rabbit,
boasting homage her lovers sprayed,

have failed her like an old
hanging bridge that decays
letting her drop through in terror

to the cold swift river beneath.
In her ears is her blood rushing.
The light is trickling away.

2.
One day this week my father
briefly emerged from the burrow
he bought himself lined with nurses.

When he gets me on the phone
he never believes it's me.
When I insist, he swells with anger.

He really wants to phone my mother.
Often he calls me by her name
but every time I fail him.

I am the dead woman in body,
hips and breasts and thighs,
elbows and chin and earlobes,

black black hair as at the age
she bore me, when he still
loved her, here she stands,

but when I open my mouth
it's the wrong year and the world
bristles with women who make short

hard statements like men and don't
apologize enough, who don't cry
when he yells or makes a fist.

He tells me I have stolen his stamps
down in Florida, the bad utopia
where he must share a television.

You took my nail scissors, he shouts
but means I stole his vigor
deposited in his checkbook like a giant's

external soul. I have his checkbook
and sign, power of attorney,
as I pay his doctors, doctors,

doctors, as I hunch with calculator
trying to balance accounts. We each
feel enslaved to the other's will.

3.
Father, I don't want your little pot
of nuggets secreted by bad living
hidden in the mattress of Merrill Lynch

in an account you haven't touched
for twenty years, stocks that soared,
plummeted, doddering along now

in their own mad dinosaur race.
That stock is the doctor that Mother
couldn't call when she had the first

stroke, the dress she didn't get,
at eighty-six still scrubbing, cooking,
toting heavy laundry. The dentist

I couldn't go to so I chewed
aspirin as my teeth broke
at fifteen when I went out to work,

all the pleasures, the easing of pain
you could have bought with both
your endless hard mutual labor.

The ghostly dust bowl roared in the mind
afterward, the desert of want
where you would surely perish and starve

if you did not hide away pennies of power,
make do, make do, hold hard,
build a fortress of petrified dollars

stuck together like papier-mâché
so the tempest of want
could be shut out to howl at others.

Dirty little shacks, a roominghouse Mother ran for decades,
a trailer park; after she died

you bought into Total Life Care,
a tower of middle class comfort
where you could sit down to lunch

declaring, my broker says.
But nobody would listen. Only
Mother had to listen and she is dead.

You hid alone in your room fighting
with the cleaning woman who came
each week but didn't do it right,

then finally one midnight wandered out naked
finally to the world among rustling
palms demanding someone make you lunch.

4.
I wouldn't sign papers to commit
you but they found a doctor who would.
Now you mutter around the ward,

This was supposed to be fun.
Do you see your future in the bent
ones who whimper into their laps,

who glare at walls through which
the faces of the absent peer, who hear
conspiracy mutter in the plumbing?

I am the bad daughter who could speak
with my mother's voice if I wanted,
because I wear her face, who ought

to be cooking your meals, who ought
to be running the vacuum you bought
her, but instead I pretend

I am married, pretend to be writing
books and giving speeches.
You won't forgive her ever for dying

but I heard you call the night nurse
by her name. You speak of the fog
you see in the room. Greyness

is blowing in, the fog that took
my mother while you slept,
the fog that shriveled your muscles,

the fog that thickens between you
and strangers here where all
is provided and nothing is wanted.

The sun blasts on, flat and blatant.
Everything was built yesterday
but you. Nobody here remembers

the strike when you walked the picket line
joking with sleet freezing your hair,
how you stood against the flaming wall

of steel and found the cracked bearing,
how you alone could make the old turbines
turn over, how you had the wife

other men watched when she swayed
over the grass at the company picnic,
how you could drink them all witless.

You're a shadow swallowed by fog.
Through your eyes it enters your brain.
When it lifts you see only pastel

walls and then your anger standing there
gleaming like a four-hundred-horsepower car
you have lost your license to drive.

Your father's fourth heart attack

The phone cord is the umbilicus
that binds him dying, shriveled,
to you his first son.
You try to draw him to you.
You give him advice. I hear

your voice tender, careful,
admonishing, arguing.
You ask him ten polite ways
why he is killing himself
by the teaspoonful, by the drop,

by the puff. Why he eats
ashes instead of apples,
why he sucks on death's
icy dry tit, why he turns
his face into darkness.

You cajole him, a step, a step
like a father coaxing a toddler,
but he falls through your fingers
into a maze of knives giving him
his face back screaming.

Twelve hours a day he worked,
four hours commuting, up nights
in a chair by TV late show light
wolfing burnt steak and salami on rye,
counting other men's paychecks.

He lived among men with boats,
sleek men, slick men, always richer.
He bought a boat from a moneyed neighbor,

fiberglass hulled, had it repaired,
started it, roared out and sank.

No place he lived was ever right,
but he was always talking up the next
move. He quarreled with brothers,
mother, friends, son, in-laws,
everyone except the bosses he twisted

and wrung himself to please.
He was always hungry. If he ate five
sandwiches, his hunger still knocked
on his bones like a broken radiator
and he was never full.

He lived a hunger bigger than a man,
a hunger to be other, golden,
a hollowness finally now filled
with pain. He holds you in the phone
but his eyes seek the dark in the mirror.

He slips in and out of his death bed
like a suit he keeps trying on, refitting.
He grabs at a hand and speaks the wrong
name, and the hand flops cold as a fish
while he calls till hoarseness, for himself.

Magic mama

The woman who shines with a dull comfortable glow.
The woman who sweats honey, an aphid
enrolled to sweeten the lives of others.

The woman who puts down her work like knitting
the moment you speak, but somehow it gets done
secretly in the night while everyone sleeps.

The woman whose lap is wide as the Nile
delta, whose flesh is a lullaby
of goosedown petals lacking the bite

of menace real lullabies ride on
(if the bough breaks, birds
and butterflies pecking out his eyes).

Whose own eyes are soft-focus mirrors.
Whose arms are bolsters. Whose love
is laid on like the municipal water.

She is not the mother goddess, vortex
of dark and light powers with her consorts,
her hungers, her favorites, her temper

blasting the corn so it withers in its ear,
her bloody humor that sends the hunter fleeing
to be tracked and torn by his hounds,

the great door into the earth's darkness
where bones are rewoven into wheat,
who loves the hawk as she loves the rabbit.

Big mama has no power, not over herself.
The taxpayer of guilt, whatever she gives
you both agree is never enough.

She is a one-way street down which pour
parades of opulent gifts and admiration
from a three-shift factory of love.

Magic mama has to make it right, straighten
the crooked, ease pain, raise the darkness,
feed the hungry and matchmake for the lonesome

and ask nothing in return. If you win
you no longer know her, and if you lose
it is because her goodness failed you.

Whenever you create big mama from another
woman's smile, a generosity of spirit working
like yeast in the inert matter of the day,

you are stealing from a woman her own ripe
grape sweet desire, the must of her fears,
the shadow she casts into her own future

and turning her into a diaper service,
the cleaning lady of your adventure.
Who thanks a lightbulb for giving light?

Listen, your mother is not your mother.
She is herself and unmothered. It is time
to take the apron off your mind.

Landed fish

Danny dead of heart attack,
mid-forties, pretzel thin
just out of the pen for passing bad checks.
He made it as he could
and the world narrowed on him,
aluminum funnel of hot California sky.

In family my mother tells a story.
My uncle is sitting on the front steps,
it is late in the Depression,
my brother has dropped out of school.
Somehow today they got staked and the horses ran.
My uncle sits on the rickety front steps
under wisteria pale mauve and littering scent.
I climb in his lap: I say
This is my Uncle Danny, I call him Donald for short,
oh how beautiful he is,
he has green eyes like my pussycat.
A Good Humor man comes jingling and Danny carries me
to buy a green ice on a stick,
first ice burning to sweet water in the tongue
in the long Depression
with cornmeal and potatoes and beans in the house to eat.

This story is told by my mother
to show how even at four I was cunning.
Danny's eyes were milky bluegreen,
sea colors I had never known.
The eyes of my cat were yellow. I was lying
but not for gain, mama. I squirm on his lap,
I am tangling my hands in his fiberglass hair.
The hook is that it pleases him
and that he is beautiful on the steps laughing

with money in the pockets of his desperate George Raft pants.
His eyes flicker like leaves,
his laugh breaks in his throat to pieces of sun.

Three years and he will be drafted and refuse to fight.
He will rot in a stockade. He will swing an ax on his foot:
the total dropout who believed in his own luck.
I am still climbing into men's laps
and telling them how beautiful they are.
Green ices are still brief and wet and sweet.
Laughing, Danny leaves on the trolley with my brother.
He is feeling lucky, their luck is running
– like smelt, Danny – and he is hustled clean
and comes home and will not eat boiled mush.
Late, late the wall by my bed shakes with yelling.

Fish, proud nosed conman, sea eyed tomcat:
you are salted away in the dry expensive California dirt
under a big neon sign shaped like a boomerang
that coaxes Last Chance   Stop Here   Last Chance.

Sun-day poacher

My Uncle Zimmy worked the face down in the soft
coal mines that hollowed out the long ridged
mountains of Pennsylvania, where the enamel
under the spigot in the claw tub at home
was stained the color of rust from iron.

In the winter he went down before the sun
came up, and when he rose, it had sunk,
a world of darkness down in the damp,
then up in the cold where the stars burned
like the sparks you see on squinted eyes.

On Sunday he hunted, gliding over the bristly
ridges that hid the tunnels, hollow rocks
whose blasted faces were bearded by shining ice.
That was his way to the sun blessing his eyes
and the tingling air the pines electrified.

He could only go with a rifle on his shoulder.
Men couldn't just walk and look. He had
to be doing something. With tenderness he sighted
the deer and shot true, disemboweled on the spot,
the snow marked with a widening rose of blood.

He butchered there and brought home venison,
better than the wan meat of the company store.
Nothing but bones would mark the spot in three
days. In winter, every bird and beast burns
with hunger, eats or snuffs out with cold.

He walked on top of the mountains he mined within
where and how he pleased, quiet as the snow
to kill. My aunt Margaret fell in love

with him and her father mocked and threatened.
A schoolteacher marry a miner? She did, fast.

You could see the way he touched her the power
they kindled between them. It was a dance
at Monday's Corners. He roared home on the icy
roads with the whisky stoking that furnace hot.
That was how men drove: fast and often drunk.

He loved her still the year she lingered on.
Money could have saved her, of course.
A child, I ate his venison adoring him,
the strength and speed of a great black bear,
the same fatality in his embrace.

Something to look forward to

Menopause – word used as an insult:
a menopausal woman, mind or poem
as if not to leak regularly or on the caprice
of the moon, the collision of egg and sperm,
were the curse we first learned to call that blood.

I have twisted myself to praise that bright splash.
When my womb opens its lips on the full
or dark of the moon, that connection
aligns me as it does the sea. I quiver,
a compass needle thrilling with magnetism.

Yet for every celebration there's the time
it starts on a jet with the seatbelt sign on.
Consider the trail of red amoebae

crawling onto hostess's sheets to signal
my body's disregard of calendar, clock.

How often halfway up the side of a mountain,
during a demonstration with the tactical police
force drawn up in tanks between me and a toilet;
during an endless wind machine panel with four males
I the token woman and they with iron bladders,

I have felt that wetness and wanted to strangle
my womb like a mouse. Sometimes it feels cosmic
and sometimes it feels like mud. Yes, I have prayed
to my blood on my knees in toilet stalls
simply to show its rainbow of deliverance.

My friend Penny at twelve, being handed a napkin
the size of an ironing board cover, cried out
Do I have to do this from now till I die?
No, said her mother, it stops in middle age.
Good, said Penny, there's something to look forward to.

Today supine, groaning with demon crab claws
gouging my belly, I tell you I will secretly dance
and pour out a cup of wine on the earth
when time stops that leak permanently;
I will burn my last tampons as votive candles.

What's that smell in the kitchen?

All over America women are burning dinners.
It's lambchops in Peoria; it's haddock
in Providence; it's steak in Chicago;
tofu delight in Big Sur; red
rice and beans in Dallas.
All over America women are burning
food they're supposed to bring with calico
smile on platters glittering like wax.
Anger sputters on her brainpan, confined
but spewing out missiles of hot fat.
Carbonized despair presses like a clinker
from a barbecue against the back of her eyes.
If she wants to grill anything, it's
her husband spitted over a slow fire.
If she wants to serve him anything
it's a dead rat with a bomb in its belly
ticking like the heart of an insomniac.
Her life is cooked and digested,
nothing but leftovers in Tupperware.
Look, she says, once I was roast duck
on your platter with parsley but now I am Spam.
Burning dinner is not incompetence but war.

My mother's body

I.
The dark socket of the year
the pit, the cave where the sun lies down
and threatens never to rise,
when despair descends softly as the snow
covering all paths and choking roads:

then hawkfaced pain seized you
threw you so you fell with a sharp
cry, a knife tearing a bolt of silk.
My father heard the crash but paid
no mind, napping after lunch

yet fifteen hundred miles north
I heard and dropped a dish.
Your pain sunk talons in my skull
and crouched there cawing, heavy
as a great vessel filled with water,

oil or blood, till suddenly next day
the weight lifted and I knew your mind
had guttered out like the Channukah
candles that burn so fast, weeping
veils of wax down the chanukia.

Those candles were laid out,
friends invited, ingredients bought
for latkes and apple pancakes,
that holiday for liberation
and the winter solstice

when tops turn like little planets.
Shall you have all or nothing
take half or pass by untouched?

Nothing you got, Nun said the dreidl
as the room stopped spinning.

The angel folded you up like laundry
your body thin as an empty dress.
Your clothes were curtains
hanging on the window of what had
been your flesh and now was glass.

Outside in Florida shopping plazas
loudspeakers blared Christmas carols
and palm trees were decked with blinking
lights. Except by the tourist
hotels, the beaches were empty.

Pelicans with pregnant pouches
flapped overhead like pterodactyls.
In my mind I felt you die
First the pain lifted and then
you flickered and went out.

2.
I walk through the rooms of memory.
Sometimes everything is shrouded in dropcloths,
every chair ghostly and muted.

Other times memory lights up from within
bustling scenes acted just the other side
of a scrim through which surely I could reach

my fingers tearing at the flimsy curtain
of time which is and isn't and will be
the stuff of which we're made and unmade.

In sleep the other night I met you, seventeen
your first nasty marriage just annulled,
thin from your abortion, clutching a book

against your cheek and trying to look
older, trying to look middle class,
trying for a job at Wanamaker's

dressing for parties in cast off
stage costumes of your sisters. Your eyes
were hazy with dreams. You did not

notice me waving as you wandered
past and I saw your slip was showing.
You stood still while I fixed your clothes,

as if I were your mother. Remember me
combing your springy black hair, ringlets
that seemed metallic, glittering;

remember me dressing you, my seventy-year-
old mother who was my last dollbaby,
giving you too late what your youth had wanted.

3.
What is this mask of skin we wear,
what is this dress of flesh,
this coat of few colors and little hair?

This voluptuous seething heap of desires
and fears squeaking, mice turned up
in a steaming haystack with their babies?

This coat has been handed down, an heirloom
this coat of black hair and ample flesh,
this coat of pale slightly ruddy skin.

This set of hips and thighs, these buttocks,
they provided cushioning for my grandmother
Hannah, for my mother Bert and for me

and we all sat on them in turn, those major
muscles on which we walk and walk and walk
over the earth in search of peace and plenty.

My mother is my mirror and I am hers.
What do we see? Our face grown young again,
our breasts grown firm, legs lean and elegant.

Our arms quivering with fat, eyes
set in the bark of wrinkles, hands puffy,
our belly seamed with childbearing,

Give me your dress that I might try it on.
Oh it will not fit you mother, you are too fat.
I will not fit you, mother.

I will not be the bride you can dress,
the obedient dutiful daughter you would chew,
a dog's leather bone to sharpen your teeth.

You strike me sometimes just to hear the sound.
Loneliness turns your fingers into hooks
barbed and drawing blood with their caress.

My twin, my sister, my lost love,
I carry you in me like an embryo
as once you carried me.

4.
What is it we turn from, what is it we fear?
Did I truly think you could put me back inside?
Did I think I would fall into you as into a molten
furnace and be recast, that I would become you?

What did you fear in me, the child who wore
your hair, the woman who let that black hair

grow long as a banner of darkness, when you
a proper flapper wore yours cropped.

You pushed and you pulled on my rubbery
flesh, you kneaded me like a ball of dough.
Rise, rise, and then you pounded me flat.
Secretly the bones formed in the bread.

I became willful, private as a cat.
You never knew what alleys I had wandered.
You called me bad and I posed like a gutter
queen in a dress sewn of knives.

All I feared was being stuck in a box
with a lid. A good woman appeared to me
indistinguishable from a dead one
except that she worked all the time.

Your payday never came. Your dreams ran
with bright colors like Mexican cottons
that bled onto the drab sheets of the day
and would not bleach with scrubbing.

My dear, what you said was one thing
but what you sang was another, sweetly
subversive and dark as blackberries
and I became the daughter of your dream.

This is your body, ashes now
and roses, but alive in my eyes, my breasts,
my throat, my thighs. You run in me
a tang of salt in the creek waters of my blood,

you sing in my mind like wine. What you
did not dare in your life you dare in mine.

THE JUNGLE AND TUNDRA OF THE BED

Walking into love

1. WHAT FEELING IS THIS?

I could not tell
if I climbed up or down.
I could feel
that the ground
was not level
and often I stumbled.
I only knew
that the light was poor,
my hands damp
and sharp fears
sang, sang like crickets
in my throat.

2. DIFFERENCE OF AGES

As I climb above the tree line
my feet are growing numb,
blood knocks in my wrists and forehead.
Voices chitter out of gnarled bushes.
I seem to be carrying
a great many useless objects,
a saw, a globe, a dictionary,
a doll leaking stuffing,
a bouquet of knitting needles,
a basin of dried heads.
Voices sigh from calendar pages
I have lived too long to love you.
Withered and hard as a spider
I crawl among bones:
awful charnel knowledge

of failure, of death, of decay.
I am old as stone.
Who can make soup of me?
A spider-peddler with pack of self
I scrabble under a sky of shame.
I must scuttle under a rock
and hide in webs
of mocking voices.

3. MEDITATION IN MY FAVORITE POSITION

Peace, we have arrived.
The touch point
where words end
and body goes on.
That's all:
finite, all five-sensual
and never repeatable.
Know you and be known,
please you and be pleased
in act:
the antidote to shame
is nakedness together.
Words end,
body goes on
and something
small and wet and real
is exchanged.

4. A LITTLE SCANDAL

The eyes of others
measure and condemn.
The eyes of others are watches ticking no.
My friend hates you.

Between you I turn and turn
holding my arm as if it were broken.
The air is iron shavings polarized.
Faces blink on and off.
I carry words back and forth in my skirt.
They pile up in front of the chairs.
Words are bricks that seal the doors and windows.
Words are shutters on the eyes
and lead gloves on the hands.
The air is a solid block.
We cannot move.

5. THE WORDS ARE SAID, THE LOVE IS MADE

Sometimes your face
burns my eyes.
Sometimes your orange chest
scalds me.
I am loud and certain with strangers.
Your hands on the table
make me shy.
There is a bird in my chest
with wings too broad
with beak that rips me
wanting to get out.
I have called it
an idiot parrot.
I have called it
a ravening eagle.
But it sings.
Bird of no name
your cries are red and wet
on the iron air.
I open my mouth
to let you out

and your shining
blinds me.

6. BEHOLD: A RELATIONSHIP

Suddenly I see it:
the gradual ease.
I no longer know how many times.
Afternoons blur into afternoons,
evenings melt into evenings.
Almost everyone guesses –
those who don't never will.
The alarms have stopped
except in my skin.
Tigers in a closet
we learn gentleness.
Our small habits together
are strange
as crows' tears
and easy as sofas.
Sometimes, sometimes
I can ask for what I want:
I have begun to trust you.

Noon of the sunbather

The sun struts over the asphalt world
arching his gaudy plumes till the streets smoke
and the city sweats oil under his metal feet.
A woman nude on a rooftop lifts her arms:

'Men have swarmed like ants over my thighs,
held their Sunday picnics of gripe and crumb,

the twitch and nip of all their gristle traffic.
When will my brain pitch like a burning tower?
Lion, come down! explode the city of my bones.'

The god stands on the steel blue arch and listens.
Then he strides the hills of igniting air,
straight to the roof he hastens, wings outspread.
In his first breath she blackens and curls like paper.
The limp winds of noon disperse her ashes.

But the ashes dance. Each ashfleck leaps at the sun.

Juan's twilight dance

Nobody understood Juan.
Slight, amiable, he did not stand upon ceremony
but was unfailingly polite.
Men liked him: he deferred with wry grace
though his pride was sore and supple with constant use.
He was fascinated by mirrors and women's eyes.
When he spoke of the past he was always alone
half in shadow among shadowy forms.
No one in his stories had names. No one had faces.
He watched himself but did not listen to his voice.
Words were water or weapons.
He was always in love with the body that burned his eyes.
His need shone in the dark and the light, always new.
He could not bear suspense or indifference.
He had to be closed into love on the instant
while his need gleamed like a knife and the words spurted.
He never understood what the women minded.
He never could see how he cheated them
with words, the mercury words no one could grasp

as they gleamed and slipped and darted.
In the woman's eyes he saw himself.
He was compiling a woman he would have to love.
He was building a woman out of a hill of bodies.
The sadness of his closets: hundreds of arms,
thousands of hollow and deflated breasts,
necks and thighs smooth as new cars,
forests of hair waving and limp.
Why do they mind? They do not learn.
Time after time they grapple to win back from him
what gleamed in his face before:
the mask of desperate beautiful need
which each woman claims.
They chase each other through his hard flesh.
The bed is his mirror.
He spends into peace and indifference. He sleeps.
He is unfailingly polite, even with Donna Elvira
howling outside his door and breaking glass.
They always lose.

The friend

We sat across the table.
he said, cut off your hands.
they are always poking at things.
they might touch me.
I said yes.

Food grew cold on the table.
he said, burn your body.

it is not clean and smells like sex.
it rubs my mind sore.
I said yes.

I love you, I said.
That's very nice, he said
I like to be loved,
that makes me happy.
Have you cut off your hands yet?

A few ashes for Sunday morning

Uproot that burning tree of lightning struck veins.
Spine, wither like a paper match.

I'm telling you, this body could bake bread,
heat a house, cure rheumatic pains,
warm at least a bed.

Green wood won't catch
but I held against my belly a green stone
frog colored with remorse and oozing words
pressed to me till the night was fagged and wan.

Reek of charred hair clotting in my lungs.
My teeth are cinders,
cured my lecherous tongue.
Only me burnt, and warmed:
no one.

Concerning the mathematician

In the livingroom you are someplace else like a cat.
You go fathoms down into abstraction
where the pressure and the cold
would squeeze the juice from my tissues.
The diving bell of your head descends.
You cut the murk and peer at luminous
razorthin creatures who peer back,
creatures with eyes and ears sticking out of their backsides
lit up like skyscrapers or planes taking off.
You are at home, you nod,
you take notes and pictures.
You surface with a matter-of-fact pout,
obscene and full of questions and shouting for supper.
You talk to me and I get the bends.
Your eyes are bright and curious as robins
and your hands and your chest where I lay my head
are warm.

I am a light you could read by

A flame from each finger,
my hands are candelabra,
my hair stands in a torch.
Out of my mouth a long flame hovers.
Can't anyone see, handing me a newspaper?
Can't anyone see, stamping my book overdue?
I walk blazing along Sixth Avenue,
burning gas blue I buy subway tokens,
a bouquet of coals, I cross the bridge.

Invisible I singe strangers and pass.
Now I am on your street.
How your window flickers.
I come bringing my burning body
like an armful of tigerlilies,
like a votive lantern,
like a roomful of tassels and leopards and grapes
for you to come into,
dance in my burning
and we will flare up together like stars
and fall to sleep.

Doing it differently

1.
Trying to enter each other,
trying to interpenetrate and let go.
Trying not to lie down in the same old rutted bed
part rack, part cocoon.
We are bagged in habit
like clothes back from the cleaners.
The map of your veins has been studied,
your thighs have been read and reported,
a leaden mistrust of the rhetoric of tenderness
thickens your tongue.
At the worst you see old movies in my eyes.
How can I persuade you that every day we choose
to give birth, to murder or feed our friends, to die a little.

2.

You are an opening in me.
Smoke thick as pitch blows in,
a wind bearing ribbons of sweet rain,
and the sun as field of dandelions, as rusty razor blade.
Scent colors the air with tear gas, with lemon lilies.
Most of the time you are not here.
Mostly I do not touch you.
Mostly I am talking to someone else.

I crawl into you, a bee furry with greed
into the deep trumpeting throat of a crimson lily
speckled like a newly hatched robin.
I roll, heavy with nectar.
Later, I will turn this afternoon into honey
and live on it, frugally.
It will sweeten my tea.

3.

In the pit of the night our bodies merge,
dark clouds passing through each other in lightning,
the joining of rivers far underground in the stone.
I feel thick but hollow, a polyp floating on currents.
My nerves have opened wide mouths
to drink you in and sing O O on the dark
till I cannot fix boundaries where you start and I stop.
Then you are most vulnerable.
In me that nakedness does not close by day.
My quick, wound, door, my opening,
my lidless eye.

Don't you think it takes trust,
your strength, your temper always
in the room with us like a Dobermann leashed.

Touch is the primal sense –
for in the womb we swam lapped and tingling.
Fainting, practicing death, we lose
sight first, then hearing, the mouth and nose deaden
but still till the end we can touch.
I fear manipulation by that handle.

Trust flourishes like a potato plant, mostly underground:
wan flowers, dusty leaves chewed by beetles,
but under the mulch as we dig
at every node of the matted tangle
the tubers, egg-shaped and golden with translucent skin,
tumble from the dirt to feed us
homely and nourishing.

4.
The Digger Indians were too primitive,
pushed onto the sparse alkaline plateau,
to make pottery that could stand on the fire.
They used to make soup by heating an oval stone
and dropping it in the pot cracking hot.
When traders came and sold them iron kettles
the women found cooking easier
but said the soup never tasted so good again.

Soup stone
blunt, heavy in my hands,
you soak, you hold, you radiate warmth,
you can serve as a weapon,
you can be used again and again
and you give a flavor to things I could miss.

5.
Beds that are mirrors,
beds that are rotisseries where I am the barbecue,
beds that are athletic fields for the Olympic trials,

beds that are dartboards, beds that are dentist's chairs,
beds that are consolation prizes floating on chicken soup,
beds where lobotomies are haphazardly performed, beds
that ride glittering through lies like a ferris wheel,
all the beds where a woman and a man
try to steal each other's bones
and call it love.

Yet that small commitment floating on a sea of spilled blood
has meaning if we inflict it.
Otherwise we fail into dry accommodation.
What we do not remake
plays nostalgic songs on the jukebox of our guts,
and leads us into the old comfortable temptation.

6.
You lay in bed depressed, passive as butter.
I brought you a rose I had grown. You said
the rose was me, dark red and perfumed and three-quarters
    open,
soft as sometimes with embarrassment you praise my skin.
You talked of fucking the rose. Then you grew awkward;
we would never be free of roles, dominance and submission,
we slam through the maze of that pinball machine forever.

I say the rose is a place where we make love.
I am a body beautiful only when fitted with yours.
Otherwise, it walks, it lifts packages, it spades.
It is functional or sick, tired or sturdy. It serves.
Together we are the rose, full, red as the inside
of the womb and head of the penis,
blossoming as we encircle, we make that symmetrical fragrant
    emblem,
then separate into discrete workday selves.
The morning mail is true. Tomorrow's picketline is true.
And the rose, the rose of our loving

crimson and sonorous as a cellist
bowing on the curve of our spines, is true.

7.
We will be equal, we say, new man and new woman.
But what man am I equal to before the law of court or custom?
The state owns my womb and hangs a man's name on me
like the tags on dogs, my name is, property of.
The language betrays us and rots in the mouth
with its aftertaste of monastic sewers on the palate.
Even the pronouns tear my tongue with their metal plates.

You could strangle me: my hands
can't even encircle your neck.
Because I open my mouth wide and stand up roaring
I am the outlawed enemy of men.
A party means what a bullfight does to the bull.
The street is a gauntlet.
I open my mail with tongs.
All the images of strength in you, fathers and prophets and
    heroes,
pull against me, till what feels right to you
wrongs me, and there is no rest from struggle.

We are equal if we make ourselves so, every day, every night
constantly renewing what the street destroys.
We are equal only if you open too on your heavy hinges
and let your love come freely, freely, where it will never be
    safe,
where you can never possess.

8.
When we mesh badly, with scraping and squeaking,
remember that every son had a mother
whose beloved son he was,
and every woman had a mother

whose beloved son she wasn't.
What feels natural and easy is soft murder
of each other and that mutant future
striving to break into bloom
bloody and red as the real rose.

Periodic, earthy, of a violent tenderness
it is the nature of this joining
to remain partial and episodic
yet feel total: a mountain that opens like a door
and then closes
like a mountain.

Crabs

They are light as flakes of dandruff with scrawny legs.
Like limpets they cling to the base of each curly hair,
go lurching among the underbrush for cover.
Our passions are their weathers.
Coitus is the *Santa Maria* hitting on virgin land,
an immigrant ship coming into harbor,
free homesteads for all.
Or native crabs vs. conquistadors wrestle and nip.
Or maybe they too mingle.
As the boat glides in, there they are, the native crabs
with mandolins and bouquets of bougainvillea
swaying on the dock singing Aloha.
For three generations we haven't seen a new face.
O the boredom, the stale genes, the incest.
Or perhaps when the two shores approach
the crabs line up to leap the gap like monkeys,
the hair always lusher on the other side.

They travel as fast as gossip.
They multiply like troubles.
They cling and persist through poison and poking and picking,
dirt and soap, torrents and drought,
like love or any other stubborn itch.

The thrifty lover

At the last moment you decided
to take the bus
rather than the plane,
to squander those hours
staring at your reflection
on a dark pane.

Then all night you rummaged
my flesh for some body else.
You pinched and kneaded
testing for ripeness, rot,
suspicious and about to reject me
or knock down the price.

You lectured me like a classroom
on your reading of the week,
used homilies, reconditioned anecdotes,
jokes with rebuilt transmissions.
All the time your eyes veered.
What's wrong, I would ask?

Nothing, you'd answer, eyes full
of nothing. He goes through women
quickly, a friend says, and now

I see how you pass through,
in a sealed train
leaving a hole like a tunnel.

All clear

Loss is also clearance.
Emptiness is also receptivity.
No, I cannot pretend:
the cells of my body lack you
and keen their specific hunger.
Yet, a low yellow sun slants over this bleak landscape
a burning kite caught in the branches.
There is a lightness in me, the absence
of the weight of your judgment
bearing on my nape,
the slow stain of your judgment
rusting the moment.
I go out with empty hands
and women touch me, casually, while we talk.
The words, the problems, the sharp faces
jostle like winter birds at a feeding station
although the crumpled fields look deserted.
I stroll in the cold gelid morning.

When it becomes clear I am not replacing you
don't think it is primarily
because you cannot be replaced.
Consider that I am taking pleasure
in space, visited but unoccupied
for every man I have loved
was like an army.

We become new

How it feels to be touching
you: an Io moth, orange
and yellow as pollen,
wings through the night
miles to mate,
could crumble in the hand.

Yet our meaning together
is hardy as an onion
and layered.
Goes into the blood like garlic.
Sour as rose hips,
gritty as whole grain,

fragrant as thyme honey.
When I am turning slowly
in the woven hammocks of our talk,
when I am chocolate melting into you,
I taste everything new
in your mouth.

You are not my old friend.
How did I used to sit
and look at you? Now
though I seem to be standing still
I am flying flying flying
in the trees of your eyes.

Burying blues for Janis

Your voice always whacked me right on the funny bone
of the great-hearted suffering bitch fantasy
that ruled me like a huge copper moon with its phases
until I could, partially, break free.
How could I help but cherish you for my bad dreams?
Your voice would grate right on the marrow-filled bone
that cooks up that rich stew of masochism where we swim,
that woman is born to suffer, mistreated and cheated.
We are trained to that hothouse of ripe pain.
Never do we feel so alive, so in character
as when we're walking the floor with the all-night blues.
When some man not being there who's better gone
becomes a lack that swells up to a gaseous balloon
and flattens from us all thinking and sensing and purpose.

Oh, the downtrodden juicy longdrawn female blues:
you throbbed up there with your face slightly swollen
and your barbed hair flying energized and poured it out,
the blast of a furnace of which the whole life is the fuel.
You embodied that good done-in mama who gives and gives
like a fountain of boozy chicken soup to a rat race of men.
You embodied the pain hugged to the breasts like a baby.
You embodied the beautiful blowzy gum of passivity,
woman on her back to the world endlessly hopelessly raggedly
offering a brave front to be fucked.
That willingness to hang on the meathook and call it love,
that need for loving like a screaming hollow in the soul,
that's the drug that hangs us and drags us down
deadly as the icy sleet of skag that froze your blood.

The Lansing bad penny come again blues

So you turn up like an old
arrest record, so you turn
up like a single boot
after I finally threw the other
away, so you turn up
like a drunken wobbly angel
making your fierce annunciation
to this wilting female
trouble, garlands of trouble.

Tomorrow you go to jail
and tonight you sit before me
brushing me with the gaze
of your eyes burning
and smoky: your eyes that
change, grey into blue,
and that look that never changes.

*Lately I haven't thought
of you every day, lately it hasn't
been as bad*, you say, and
when I laugh, your mouth
calls me cruel.

Ah, you chew your heart
like a steak rare and salty.
When you are cozy in my bed
you twitch with restlessness,
you want to be mirroring your
face in shop windows in Port
au Prince. When you are gone
a thousand miles you wake up
with the veins of your arm

boring like sirens, and you
want me night and morning
till your belly wrings dry.

I am simple and dogged
as a turtle crossing a road
while you dance jagged epicycles
around me. Now you are
laughing because you know
how to unzip shells. For a few
hours we will both get
just what we want: this is Act
Forty-Four in a play
that would be tedious to observers
but for us strict
and necessary as a bullfight,
a duel, the dance of double
suns, twinned stars
whose attraction and repulsion
balance as they inscribe
erratic orbits whose center
is where the other was
or will be.

Snow in May

It isn't supposed to happen:
snow on the apple boughs
beside the blossoms, the hills
green and white at once.
Backs steaming, horses
stand in the crusted pasture
switching their tails
in the snow, their broad
flanks like doors of leather
ovens. We lie on a mattress
in the high room with no
heat. Your body chills.
I keep taking parts of you
into my mouth, finny nose,
ears like question marks,
fatfaced toes, raspberry
cock, currant nipples, plum
balls. The snow hangs
sheets over the windows.

My grandmother used to drink
tea holding a sugar cube
between her teeth: hot boiling
strong black tea
from a glass. A gleaming
silver spoon stood up.
Before we make a fire of
our bodies I braid my black
hair and I am Grandmother braiding
her greystreaked chestnut hair
rippling to her waist before
she got into bed with me

to sleep, dead now
half my life. Ice on the palm
of my hand melting,
so cold it burns me.

The back pockets of love

Your toes:
   modest stalagmites
      sticking up in the ice caves
         of the winter bed.

Your toes:
   succulent mushrooms,
      stumpy chimney pots
         rising in their row.

Wee round faces
   anonymous as nuns,
      callused, worn as coolies
         aging in their traces.

Small fry,
   wriggling moonbeam
      minnows escaped from the dark
         traps of your shoes.

Pipsqueak puppets,
   piglets nosing,
      soft thimbles, dumpy
         sofa pillows of flesh.

Love dwells in the major caves of the psyche,
chewing on the long bones of the limbs of courage,

the great haunches of resolution,
sucking the marrow bones, caverns lit
by the lasting flames of the intellect,

but love cherishes too the back pockets,
the pencil ends of childhood fears,
the nose picking and throbbing sweet tooth,
the silly hardworking toes that curl
now blamelessly as dwarf cats
in the warm covers of the sweet
tousled nest of mutual morning bed.

The homely war

1.
Wrote two letters while rain
trickled in lean streaks down my window.
One crowed of friends hiking, steamers, hot pie,
fat with bobwhite, peas planted and rhubarb dug in.
There are facts offered in the hand like ripe raspberries,
common phrases gentle as the caress of trailing hair.

The other malingered in a recitativo of wrongs,
counterpoint of minor and major abuse
quavering on a few tones of No.
A defense after my execution, a sense
that catches on the lip like a chipped glass
of having been used: used like a coin in a slot
or a borrowed towel slung sopping on a chair.
Tanglement that broke raw, in physical threat.
Months later the lies still come back
letters battered and stained, from a false address.

Happiness is simple
a box of sunshine
body against body, closed circuit of response.
Only misery is so complicated.

When another year turns over
compost in the pile
last year's feast breeding knots of juicy worms,
I do not want to be indicting
new accusations to another exlover
who has thrown off the scarlet cloak of desire to reveal
the same skeletal coldness, the need to control
flashing like a calculator in his eyes,
the eggshell ego and the sandpaper touch,
the boyish murderer spitting mommy on his bayonet.
I am tired of finding my enemy in my bed.

2.
For two years I broke from these cycles, simply.
I thought the death of sex would quiet the air to crystal.
I would see what there was between women and men
besides itch, dependency, habit.

I learned less than I expected.
Judgment sat on my shoulder like a pet crow.
My dreams were skim milk and albumin.
I lacked irrational joy, a lion
lying on my chest purring, the hawk's talons and cry,
the coarse glory of the daylily that every midsummer morning
raises a new trumpet, that withers with dusk.
My head was severed like a flower in a glass
that would never make seeds.
Like an oak my tap goes deep,
more of me is in the earth than spread into air.
I think best rooted grappling past words.

Better, I thought, for me in my rough being
to force makeshift connections,
patches, encounters, rows,
better to swim in trouble like a muddy river rising
than to become at last all thesis
correct, consistent but hollow
the finished ghost
of my own struggle.

3.
Madeline, in your purity I find myself rebuked.
Madeline, in your clarity I find myself restored.
You are the stream that breaks out
of a living tree; like the peach
you open your blossoms
to the wind that bears frost
a knife in its teeth,
you bloom in a ravaged landscape
black spring
old deaths coming to light
bones and split bellies of hunger,
the remaindered pages of the fall.
You stand and open from bare wood
fertile alone like the peach tree.
Long delicate leaves, slim green moons
ripple over the sweet fruit
rounding on its stones.

You strike on marble at the core, rock
metamorphosed in pain and pressure,
the texture of agonized flesh.
You are vulnerable as the first buds of the maple
the deer arch their necks to crop.

Delicacy and honesty, unicorn and amazon wrestle
in your high sugar maple forest,

the Vermont hillside you love,
hard wood that drips sweetness you mistrust,
the symmetrical sculpture of each leaf,
the dome of the summer tree
heavy and dense as syrup, as sleep.

You grow deep into your rock, down into the cold
crevices of the fear of first and last things.
The stone of your death you crack and enter
with your lightning brain, with your fingers that ache.
Pain is the familiar whispering in your ear.

I come with my raggedy loves dragging
into the sphere of your clear regard.
I praise our common fight.
I praise friendship embarked on suddenly as a bus that arrives.
I praise friendship maturing like a tall beech tree.
I praise the differences that define us.
I love what I cannot be
as well as what I am.

4.
Seeking from women nurturance, feedback, idea,
my politics, my collective, why then this
open frontier with men? Yet I tell you in the other
I meet the dream exotic as a dragonfly's eye,
the grenade of a phrase, the joke that would never
leap the gap of the poles of my mind,
the angers struck unexpected
a spade clanging on rock in sand.
Talking without words on the body's drum:
it is flat, it is woody, it is lean as a shark's belly,
spiny as a sea urchin, leathery, gross, tulip sleek,
fur of the hair or wool of the sheep,
the toadstool of sex raising its ruddy bald head.
I find you beautiful, I find you funny, I find

you not translatable to words of my blood.
In that meeting I seep
out to the limits where my ego fades
into flesh, into electricity of the muscles thrumming,
into light patterns imploding on the nerves,
into the wet caves where my strength is born again.

I never want to merge: only to overlap,
to grow sensitive in the moment so that we move
together as currents, so that carried
on that wave we sense skin upon skin
nerve into nerve with millions of tiny windows
open to each other's light as we shine
from the nebulous center like squid
and then let go.

5.
My old friend, how we sustain
each other, how we bear witness.
We are each other's light luggage of essentials.
We are each other's film archive and museum
packed in the crumbling arch of the skull.
Trust is the slowest strength, growing
microscopic ring on ring of living wood.
The greater gift is caring,
the laying on of hands in the dark,
of words in the light.
The lesser gift is remembering,
compass in the bush that makes clear the way
come, the way to go.

My new friend, every beginning throws the scent
of a sunny morning in a pine grove after rain.
The senses stretch out the necks of giraffes
for the smallest leaf of data to understand.
We give with the doors wide open;

a gardener with too many tomatoes,
we count nothing, we fill bushels with joy.
When does the tallying start?
Slowly underground fears begin, invisible
as the mycelium of a toadstool
waiting only for a damp morning to sprout.
I ask you to give much, to give up more.
What comes easy to a man comes
out of women. Nothing will be easy here.
Good will starts out fat and sweet
as tub butter and turns slowly rancid.
It must be made again daily
if we want it fresh.

6.
I am sick, sick to desperation
of the old defeats, of the broken treaties,
episodes of the same colonial war of women and men.
I want the cavalry to take off those bemedaled blue uniforms
the colour of Zeus and those shiny boots clanking with spurs.
I want the horses to win this time and eat grass together.

In this movie the Army always comes bugling over the hill,
burns some squaws and pens up the rest on a reservation,
paves over the sacred dancing ground for a Stop and Shop,
and a ten-lane turnpike to the snowmobile factory.
Then they ask the doctor why nothing is fun.
Their eyes are the color of television screens.
They come by pretending, they die with their minds turned off.

Do you think on the tenting ground of General Bluster
young renegades may begin to steal away?
Or will they always go back for their paychecks?
I think it is time for the extras to burn down the movie.

Yes, I am sick of treaties with the enemy who brings to bed
his boots and his law, who is
still and after my enemy.
I have been trained to love him, and he to use me.
Yes, I am weary of war where I want exchange,
sick of harvesting disgust from the shoots of joy.
Fight with my tribe or die in your blue uniform
but don't think you can take it off in bed.
It dyes your words, your brain runs cobalt
and your tear ducts atrophy to pebbles.

I love easily: never mind that.
Love is the paper script of this loose army.
Let us sleep on honesty at night like a board.
Talk with your body, talk with your life.
Grow me good will
rough and thick as meadow grass
but tend it like an invalid house plant,
a tender African violet in the best window.

A story wet as tears

Remember the princess who kissed the frog
so he became a prince? At first they danced
all weekend, toasted each other in the morning
with coffee, with champagne at night
and always with kisses. Perhaps it was
in bed after the first year had ground
around she noticed he had become cold
with her. She had to sleep
with a heating pad and down comforter.
His manner grew increasingly chilly
and damp when she entered a room.
He spent his time in water sports,
hydroponics, working on his insect
collection.

      Then in the third year
when she said to him one day, my dearest,
are you taking your vitamins daily,
you look quite green, he leaped
away from her.

      Finally on their
fifth anniversary she confronted him.
'My precious, don't you love me any
more?' He replied, 'Rivet. Rivet.'
Though courtship turns frogs into princes,
marriage turns them quietly back.

It breaks

You hand me a cup of water;
I drink it and thank you pretending
what I take into me so calmly
could not kill me. We take food
from strangers, from restaurants
behind whose swinging doors flies
swarm and settle, from estranged
lovers who dream over the salad plates
of breaking the bones of our backs
with a sledgehammer.

Trust flits through the apple
blossoms, a tiny spring warbler
in bright mating plumage. Trust
relies on learned pattern
and signal to let us walk down
stairs without thinking each
step, without stumbling.

I breathe smog and pollen
and perfume. I take parts
of your body inside me. I give you
the flimsy black lace and sweat
stained sleaze of my secrets.
I lay my sleeping body naked
at your side. Jump, you shout.
I do and you catch me.

In love we open wide as a house
to a summer afternoon, every shade up
and window cranked open and doors
flung back to the probing breeze.
If we love for long, we stand like row

houses with no outer walls
on the companionable side.

Suddenly we are naked,
abandoned. The plaster of bedrooms
hangs exposed to the street, wall
paper, pink and beige skins of broken
intimacy torn and flapping.

To fear you is fearing my left
hand cut off, a monstrous crab
scaling the slippery steps of night.
The body, the lineaments of old
desire remain, but the gestures
are new and harsh. Words unheard
before are spat out grating
with the rush of loosed anger.

Friends bear back to me banner
headlines of your rewriting of our
common past. You explain me away,
a dentist drilling a tooth.
I wonder at my own trust, how absolute
it was, mortal but part of me
like the bones of my pelvis.
You were the true center of my
cycles, the magnetic north
I used to plot my wanderings.

It is not that I will not love
again or give myself into partnership
or lie naked sweating secrets
like nectar, but I will never
share a joint checking account
and when some lover tells me, *Always,
baby*, I'll be thinking, sure,
until this one meets an heiress

and ships out. After a bone breaks
you can see in X rays
the healing and the damage.

In the wet

How you shine from the inside
orange as a pumpkin's belly,
your face beautiful as children's
faces when they want
at white heat, when fear pinches
them, when they have not learned
how to lie well
yet.

Your pain flows into me through
my ears and fingers. Your pain
presses in, I cannot keep it away.
Like a baby in my body
you kick me as you stretch
and knock the breath out.

Yet when I shook with pain's
fever, when fear chewed me
raw all night, you held me, you
held on. Then I was the baby
past words and blubbering.
The words, the comfort were yours
and you nurtured me shriveled

like a seed that would
never uncurl.

How strangely we mother each
other, sister and brother, lovers,
twins. For you to love me means
you must love yourself.
That is what loving is, I say,
it is not pain, it is not
pleasure, it is not compulsion
or fantasy. It is only a way
of living, wide open.

September afternoon at four o'clock

Full in the hand, heavy
with ripeness, perfume spreading
its fan: moments now resemble
sweet russet pears glowing
on the bough, peaches warm
from the afternoon sun, amber
and juicy, flesh that can
make you drunk.

There is a turn in things
that makes the heart catch.
We are ripening, all the hard
green grasping, the stony will
swelling into sweetness, the acid
and sugar in balance, the sun
stored as energy that is pleasure
and pleasure that is energy.

Whatever happens, whatever,
we say, and hold hard and let
go and go on. In the perfect
moment the future coils,
a tree inside a pit. Take,
eat, we are each other's
perfection, the wine of our
mouths is sweet and heavy.
Soon enough comes the vinegar.
The fruit is ripe for the taking
and we take. There is
no other wisdom.

The infidelity of sleep

We tie our bodies in a lover's
knot and then gradually uncoil.
We turn and talk, the night lapping
at the sills of the casements, rising
in us like dark heavy wine.

Then we turn aside. Eskimo
crawling into private igloos,
bears retreating to distant lairs,
a leopard climbing its home tree,
we go unmated into sleep.

In sleep you fret about who a lover
untouched for years is sleeping with.
Some man with a face glimpsed once

in a crowd lies over me sweating.
Now I wear male flesh like a suit of armor.

In sleep I am speaking French again.
The Algerian War is still on.
I curse, back to the wall of the top
floor of a workers'-quarter house.
The war in Vietnam is still on.

I am carrying a memorized message
to a deserter who is hiding
in a church belfry. All night
I drive fast down back roads
with a borrowed car full of contraband.

In the mornings, of what we remember,
what can we tell? In the mind
dreams flash their faces, but in words
they dim, brilliant rocks picked up
at low tide that dry to mud.

Nightly the tides of sleep enter
us in secret claret-red oceans
from whose deep slide serpents
wearing faces radiant and impure
as saints in Renaissance paintings.

Now as night pours in to fill the house
like a conch shell, we cling together,
muttered words between us, a spar
we hold to knowing that soon
we will let go, severed, to drown.

The faithless

Sleep, you jade smooth liar,
you promised to come
to me, come to me
waiting here like a cut
open melon ripe as summer.

Sleep, you black velvet
tomcat, where are you prowling?
I set a trap of sheets
clean and fresh as daisies,
pillows like cloudy sighs.

Sleep, you soft bellied
angel with feathered thighs,
you tease my cheek with the brush
of your wings. I reach
for you but clutch air.

Sleep, you fur bottomed tramp,
when I want you, you're in
everybody's bed but my own.
Take you for granted and you stalk
me from the low point of every hour.

Sleep, omnivorous billygoat,
you gobble the kittens, the crows,
the cop on duty, the fast horse
but me you leave on the plate
like a cold shore dinner.

Is this divorce permanent?
Runneled with hope I lie down
nightly longing to pass

again under the fresh blessing
of your weight and broad wings.

Sexual selection among birds

The soft breasted dun bird on her nest
incubating a clutch of sand colored eggs,
her dreams are scarlet and cobalt.

Her mate is gaudy, enameled like
a Fabergé egg, jeweled and singing:
the artifact of her aesthetic lust.

Over the bower of bush where she waits
he dances in the air, mine, mine:
but she knows better.

Of all the females, she, feathered
dinosaur, is the choosiest, the most
critical, demanding of her mate

not only fidelity, passion, offspring
but that he sing like Mozart
and bloom like a perfect rose.

It arrives suddenly and carries us off as usual

Sometimes in early June I am standing
under the just unpacked green of the oak
when a hot bearish paw suddenly flattens the air:
a warm front marches in palpable as
a shove, a sudden fanfare from the brass.

I am putting dishes away in the cupboard.
You are screwing a bulb into the fixture:
is it the verb, the analogy, the mischievous
child of the limbic brain fitting shards together?
We both think of sex as if a presence

had entered the room, a scent of salt
and hot feathers, a musky tickle
along the spine like arpeggios
galloping down the scale to the bass
that resonates from skull to soles.

The body that has been functioning,
a tidy machine, retracts its armor
of inattention and the skin shimmers
with mouths of light crying let me take
you in, I must be laved in touch.

Now, now. Five minutes later
we are upstairs, the phone out of the wall,
doors locked, clothes tossed like casualties
through three rooms. We are efficient
in our hunger, neat as a sharpshin stooping.

Half an hour after that we are back,
me at the cupboard, you on the ladder,
our clothes rumpled, reeking of secretions

and satisfaction, dazed as if carried
to a height and dropped straight down.

On guard

I want you for my bodyguard,
to curl round each other like two socks
matched and balled in a drawer.

I want you to warm my backside,
two S's snaked curve to curve
in the down burrow of the bed.

I want you to tuck in my illness,
coddle me with tea and chicken
soup whose steam sweetens the house.

I want you to watch my back
as the knives wink in the thin light
and the whips crack out from shelter.

Guard my body against dust and disuse,
warm me from the inside out,
lie over me, under me, beside me

in the bed as the night's creek
rushes over our shining bones
and we wake to the morning fresh

and wet, a birch leaf just uncurling.
Guard my body from disdain as age
widens me like a river delta.

Let us guard each other until death,
with teeth, brain and galloping heart,
each other's rose red warrior.

Implications of one plus one

Sometimes we collide, tectonic plates merging,
continents shoving, crumpling down into the molten
veins of fire deep in the earth and raising
tons of rock into jagged crests of Sierra.

Sometimes your hands drift on me, milkweed's
airy silk, wingtip's feathery caresses,
our lips grazing, a drift of desires gathering
like fog over warm water, thickening to rain.

Sometimes we go to it heartily, digging,
burrowing, grunting, tossing up covers
like loose earth, nosing into the other's
flesh with hot nozzles and wallowing there.

Sometimes we are kids making out, silly
in the quilt, tickling the xylophone spine,
blowing wet jokes, loud as a whole
slumber party bouncing till the bed breaks.

I go round and round you sometimes, scouting,
blundering, seeking a way in, the high boxwood
maze I penetrate running lungs bursting
toward the fountain of green fire at the heart.

Sometimes you open wide as cathedral doors
and yank me inside. Sometimes you slither

into me like a snake into its burrow.
Sometimes you march in with a brass band.

Ten years of fitting our bodies together
and still they sing wild songs in new keys.
It is more and less than love: timing,
chemistry, magic and will and luck.

One plus one equal one, unknowable except
in the moment, not convertible into words,
not explicable or philosophically interesting.
But it is. And it is. And it is. Amen.

HOUSE BUILT ON A SANDBAR

The ark of consequence

The classic rainbow shows as an arc,
a bridge strung in thinning clouds,
but I have seen it flash a perfect circle,
rising and falling and rising again
through the octave of colors,
a sun shape rolling like a wheel of light.

Commonly it is a fraction of a circle,
a promise only partial, not a banal
sign of safety like a smile pin,
that rainbow cartoon affixed to vans
and baby carriages. No, it promises
only, this world will not self-destruct.

Account the rainbow a boomerang of liquid
light, foretelling rather that what we
toss out returns in the water table;
flows from the faucet into our bones.
What we shoot up into orbit falls
to earth through the roof one night.

Think of it as a promise that what
we do continues in an arc
of consequence, flickers in our
children's genes, collects in each
spine and liver, gleams in the apple,
coats the down of the drowning duck.

When you see the rainbow iridescence
shiver in the oil slick, smeared
on the waves of the poisoned river,
shudder for the covenant broken, for we
are given only this floating round ark
with the dead moon for company and warning.

Gracious goodness

On the beach where we had been idly
telling the shell coins
cat's paw, cross-barred Venus, china cockle,
we both saw at once
the sea bird fall to the sand
and flap grotesquely.
He had taken a great barbed hook
out through the cheek and fixed
in the big wing.
He was pinned to himself to die,
a royal tern with a black crest blown back
as if he flew in his own private wind.
He felt good in my hands, not fragile
but muscular and glossy and strong,
the beak that could have split my hand
opening only to cry
as we yanked on the barbs.
We borrowed a clippers, cut and drew out the hook.
Then the royal tern took off, wavering,
lurched twice,
then acrobat returned to his element, dipped,
zoomed and sailed out to dive for a fish.
Virtue: what a sunrise in the belly.
Why is there nothing
I have ever done with anybody
that seems to be so obviously right?

The road behind the last dune

(from *Sand Roads*)

Mostly you don't see the ocean
although when the surf is up
its roaring fills you
like a shell
whistling through your ears,
your bones.

Nothing stands up here
but you, in the steady
rasp of the salt wind.
The oaks grow a foot high
dry gnarled jungles
you can't wade through
where eyes watch.
The hog cranberry bronze
in the fall, shines
metallically revealing
every hump.
The dune grass ripples
like a pelt, and around
every clump is traced a circle,
fingers of the wind.
Fox grape on the high dunes,
poison ivy whose bright berries
the birds carry in their bodies
to scatter seed, the dune
colored grasshoppers,
the fox with fur of fine sand.

You are standing too tall for
this landscape. Lie down.
Let the grass blow

over you. Let the plover pipe,
the kestrel stand beating its wings
in the air, the wolf spider
come to the door of its burrow,
the mouse nibble on
your toe. Let the beach pea
entangle your legs in its vine
and ring you with purple blossoms.

Now get up slowly
and seek a way down off the dunes
carefully: your heavy feet
assault the balance.
Come down on the bench
of the great beach arching
away into fog.
Lie down before the ocean.
It rises over you, it stands
hissing and spreading its
cobalt hood, rattling
its pebbles.
Cold it is and its rhythm
as it eats away the beach,
as it washes the dunes out to sea
to build new spits and islands,
enters your blood and slows
the beat of that newish contraption
your heart controlling the waves
of your inward salt sea.
Let your mind open
like a clam when the waters
slide back to feed it.
Flow out to the ancient cold
mothering embrace, cold
and weightless yourself

as a fish, over the buried
wrecks. Then with respect
let the breakers drive you
up and out into
the heavy air, your heart
pounding. The warm scratchy sand
like a receiving blanket
holds you up gasping with life.

Doors in the wind and the water

Doors open in the mind
and close again like wounds
healing. Doors open in the
mind and close again like
dying fish whose gills fall
finally still. Doors in the mind
open and close like mountains
you see spired white past other
mountains but never reach.

Doors open flashing in the sundarkened wave,
doors in the brown carp pool,
doors in the beard of the waterfall,
doors in the green caverns
of the tree, doors in the eye
of the goat, of the alley cat,
doors in the hand held up,
doors in the astonished skin.

The self is last summer's
clothes unpacked from suitcases.
The self is your old physics

notebook filled with experiments
you had to fake. A well thumbed
deck where the joker fills in
for the King of Diamonds
and the dog has eaten the Ace
of Spades, but there
are five battered sevens.

Always too at the root tips growing
or dying, dark osmotic exchange
of particles, of energy, of dreams
goes wetly on. The larger mysteries
come to us at morning and evening
crowned with bladderwrack and gull feathers,
wearing the heads of cows, of horned owls,
of our children who are not ours,
of strangers whose faces open
like doors where we enter
or flee.

Of the patience called forth by transition

Notice how the sky is a milky opal
cloudless from rim to rim, of an indefinite
height and sliding now at midafternoon
into darkness. Pearly, it melts
imperceptibly into yellow and green,
willow colors from another season,
or the yellow of aspen leaves already fallen,
into lavender now, the sea lavender
shriveled in the marshes. As the trees
reduce themselves to bony gesture
and the woods echo the hues of earth
itself, the colors of light must feed
our eye's hunger, the ruddy sun of winter.

In early spring, we look down for color,
we look for the green of skunk cabbage,
golden crocuses along the south walls,
the small ears of violets unfolding.
Before the snows that glaze and magnify,
glitter and transmute, we look upwards.
Great Chinese peonies float over the bay
splendid, bronzed by the light rebounding
from the water. In November we gaze up
into the stormy garden of the clouds.
What comes to us rides on the wind
and we face into it like gulls, waiting.

Snow, snow

Like the sun on February ice dazzling;
like the sun licking snow back
roughly so objects begin to poke through,
logs and steps, withered clumps of herb;
like the torch of the male cardinal
borne across the clearing from pine
to pine and then lighting among the bird
seed and bread scattered; like the sharp
shinned hawk gliding over the rabbit
colored marsh grass, exulting
in talon hooked cries to his larger mate;
like the little pale green seedlings sticking
up their fragile heavy heads on white stalks
into the wide yellow lap of the pregnant sun;
like the sky of stained glass the eye seeks
for respite from the glitter that makes the lips
part; similar to all these pleasures
of the failing winter and the as yet unbroken
blue egg of spring is our joy as we twist
and twine about each other in the bed
facing the window where the sun plays
the tabla of the thin cold air
and the snow sings soprano
while the emerging earth drones bass.

How grey, how wet, how cold

They are bits of fog caught in armor.
The outside pretends to the solidity of rocks
and requires force and skill bearing in
to cut the muscle, shatter the illusion.

If you stare at them, your stomach
curls, the grey eyes of Athena
pried out, the texture of heavy phlegm,
chill clots of mortality and come.

They lie on the tongue, distillations
of the sea. Fresh as the morning
wind that tatters the mist.
Sweet as cream but with that bottom

of granite, the taste of deep well
water drawn up on the hottest day,
the vein of slate in true Chablis,
the kiss of acid sharpening the tongue.

They slip down quick as minnows
darting to cover, and the mouth
remembers sex. Both too provide
a meeting of the primitive

and worldly, in that we do
little more for oysters than the gull
smashing the shells on the rocks
or the crab wrestling them open,

yet in subtle flavor and the choice
to taste them raw, comes a delicacy
not of the brain but of the senses
and the wit to leave perfection bare.

This small and intimate place

1.
The moor land, the dry land ripples
bronzed with blueberry. The precise
small hills sculpted with glittering
kinnickinnick bake under the sharp
tack of the redtailed hawk cruising
in middle air. A vesper sparrow
gives its repetitive shrill sad cry
and the air shimmers with drought.

The sea is always painting itself
on the sky, which dips low here.
Light floods the eyes tight and dry.
Light scours out the skull
like an old kitchen sink made clean.
We are cured in sunlight like salt cod.

2.
We are cured in sunlight like salt cod
stiffened and rot repellent and long
lived, long lasting. The year-rounders
are poor. All summer they wait tables
for the tourists, clean the houses
of the summer people, sell them jam, fish,
paintings, build their dwellings, wait
for the land to be clean and still again.

Yet blueberries, black- and elderberries,
beachplum grow where vacation homes
for psychiatrists are not yet built.
We gather oysters, dig clams. We burn
oak, locust, pitchpine and eat much fish
as do the other scavengers, the gulls.

3.
As do the other scavengers, the gulls
we suffer, prey on the tides' rise and ebb
of plenty and disaster, the slick that chokes
the fisheries, the restaurant sewage
poisoning mussels, the dump leaching lead
into the water table; the lucky winter
storm that tosses up surf clams or squid
in heaps for food, fertilizer, future plenty.

This land is a tablet on which each pair
of heels writes itself, the raw scar
where the dirt bike crossed, the crushed
tern chicks where the ORV roared through,
the dune loosed over trodden grasses.
We are intimate with wind and water here.

4.
We are intimate with wind. Once
this was a land of windmills flapping
sails like a stationary race of yachts.
We learn the winds on face and shingles,
the warm wind off the gulf stream in winter,
the nor'easter piling up snow and wrecks,
the west wind that hustles the rain clouds
over and out to sea, the cold northwest.

We are intimate with water, lapped around,
the sea tearing at the land, castling it up,
damp salty days with grey underworld light
when sneakers mold like Roquefort, paper wilts.
On moors webbed in fog we wander, or wade
in the salt marsh as the wetlands ripple.

Moon of the mother turtle

I am the busybody who interferes.
All through turtle mating season
I am hauling the females out of the road
and setting them where I presume
it is safe to lay their eggs.

Who appointed me guardian of turtles?
Yet when I see their bodies broken
like rotten pumpkins on the blacktop
I get so angry I have no choice but
to go on dragging them to sandbanks.

My least favorite duty is the two weeks
of snapping turtles. Occasionally I grasp
a weighty female and haul her out
of the way of cars before she can react.
Other times it's a wrestling match,

me with a stick and she with her beak,
neither of us prepared to back down,
a tug of war, wrestling, snarling
in the ruts of the old railroad right of way.
She must, she must. The eggs press

on her to be born. She is half mad.
Her eyes glitter dully as sun
glimpsed through muddy water. She is
the ancient of days raging with the urge
to dig and lay, dig and lay more.

I am a yelping dog circling, just as mad
to get her out of the roadway. She
hisses like a mother cat. Her great

beak clacks. She stinks like muck
from the basement of the fish maker's shop.

When finally I get her onto the bank, she
goes to it at once, sighing. A train
could pass a few feet away as it used to
and she would lay on. I am forgotten
as I haul two ties to build her a rampart.

Then we go our separate ways, me toward
the bay to complete my four-mile walk,
she back to Bound Brook, dragging her
massive belly, each under our compulsions
like moons with the same and different faces.

Fox grapes

It is near the railroad bridge over the creek
where wild blue grapes run rampant up trees,
the ones the locals call fox grapes.
I have seen you peck them with your teeth.

You are poised in the old right of way,
your body a straight line out to the plume's tip
but for your jack of diamond's face, pointed,
wary, jutting at me sharp as a glass corner.

Our eyes meet. We stand each with our feet
loaded and ready to discharge into motion.
That look is opaque and piercing and curious.
We drink each other like whiskey, straight

and strong and blinding in the brain.
For a long time we hold each other stabbed

through as if by desire. Then you stir
and are gone in the baked grasses. All day

nothing human of words or touch pierces my brain
to that deep spot where your ember smolders.
Your family is breaking. You start your wild
solitary fall when you hunt and run alone.

Nailing up the mezuzah

A friend from Greece
brought a tin house
on a plaque, designed
to protect our abode,
as in Greek churches
embossed legs or hearts
on display entreat aid.
I hung it but now
nail my own proper charm.

I refuse no offers of help,
at least from friends,
yet this presence
is long overdue. Mostly
we nurture our own
blessings or spoil them,
build firmly or undermine
our walls. Who are termites
but our obsessions gnawing?

Still the winds blow hard
from the cave of the sea
carrying off what they will.

Our smaller luck abides
like a worm snug in an apple
who does not comprehend
the shivering of the leaves
as the ax bites hard
in the smooth trunk.

We need all help proffered
by benign forces. Outside
we commit our beans to the earth,
the tomato plants started
in February to the care
of the rain. My little
pregnant grey cat offers
the taut bow of her belly
to the sun's hot tongue.

Saturday I watched alewives
swarm in their thousands
waiting in queues quivering
pointed against the white
rush of the torrents
to try their leaps upstream.
The gulls bald as coffin
nails stabbed them casually
conversing in shrieks, picnicking.

On its earth, this house
is oriented. We grow
from our bed rooted firmly
as an old willow into the water
of our dreams flowing deep
in the hillside. This hill
is my temple, my soul.
Moloch ha-moves, angel of death
pass over, pass on.

The cat's song

Mine, says the cat, putting out its paw of darkness.
My lover, my friend, my slave, my toy, says
the cat making on your chest his gesture of drawing
milk from his mother's forgotten breasts.

Let us walk in the woods, says the cat.
I'll teach you to read the scandal sheet of scents,
to fade into shadow, wait like a trap, to hunt.
Now I lay this plump warm mouse on your mat.

You feed me, I try to feed you, we are friends,
says the cat, although I am more equal than you.
Can you leap twenty times the height of your body?
Can you run up and down trees? Jump between roofs?

Let us rub our bodies together and talk of touch.
My emotions are pure as salt crystals and as hard.
My lusts glow like my eyes. I sing to you in the mornings
walking round and round your bed and into your face.

Come I will teach you to dance as naturally
as falling asleep and waking and stretching long, long.
I speak greed with my paws and fear with my whiskers.
Envy lashes my tail and love speaks me entire, a word

of fur. I will teach you to be still as an egg
and to slip like the ghost of wind through the grass.

Shad blow

1.
Deer tracks cloven dark in the pale sand.
The grey squirrels shriek and chase each other
crashing from branch to branch of the oaks.

The shad bloom is late this year and perfect,
trees that are one great composite flower,
wild carrots, Queen Anne's lace the size

of giraffes riffled by the breeze
miles of salt water have scrubbed
bone white. Orange and lemon orioles

flit among knotted branches. The trunks
of shad are grey, blotched with lichen,
fog caught and woven into wood.

2.
I used to lie under the sour cherry in the narrow
yard of the house where we moved the year
I turned fifteen. White galaxies that would become

wine by summer's end, pies in the sky,
flashed against the sulfurous clouds of Detroit
blossoms out of mahogany bark shining.

Who will I be? The will to love
ate holes in my mind. I was riddled
like a sieve with sharp sour desires.

I can taste that raw home made wine,
taste a sweet and sour intoxicating pain
so empty, wanting played shrilly on me

like the wind over the mouth of a bottle
compelling a keening too high pitched
for a human to notice, but the dog next

door flung back his head and howled too
and my cat came stepping through the unmown
grass to circle three times, then marked

the tree with his spray as I burned
to mark the world with something of mine.
Spring came on like cramps in a growing body.

3.
In spring I raise my head to sniff at scents.
I want to be out by the river watching the ale-
wives straddling the current, humping upstream.

I thrust my hands into the cool rich soil,
the moss like fur between the cracks of the stones.
I want to roll like a big dog and shake free.

The salamander cool as jelly, darkly colored
as cabernet sauvignon lies on my palm
then leaps to freedom, snap, in the wood pile.

Appetite licks at the air, the tiny leaves
opening their clenched silken banners.
At two in the afternoon the fox runs on the beach

going to paw at the late alewives crossing
the bar where the brook eases into the bay.
A gull runs at him, then flaps off.

Once I thought the seasons were mine,
moods, passions, itches I could scratch,
voids I could fill with other bodies.

Now I know I am in the seasons, of them.
The sun warms the upturned soil and my arm.
Spring moves through me like an armada of light.

The visitation

The yearling doe stands by the pile of salt
hay, nibbling, and then strolls up the path.
Among the spring bulbs she stands amazed,
hundreds of daffodils, forsythia,
the bright chalices of tulips, crimson,
golden, orange streaked with green, the wild
tulips opening like stars fallen on the ground.
She leans gracefully to taste a tarda,
yellow and white sunburst, sees us, stops,
uncertain. Stares at us with her head cocked.
What are you? She is not frightened
but bemused. Do I know you?
The landscaping dazzles her, impresses her
far more than the two of us on the driveway
speaking to her in the same tone as we use
with the cats as if she had become our pet,
as she sidles among the peach trees,
a pink blossom clinging to her dun flank.

Graceful among the rhododendron, I know
what her skittish courage represents: she
is beautiful as those sub-Saharan children
with the huge luminous brown eyes of star-
vation. A hard winter following a hurricane,
tangles of downed trees even the deer
cannot penetrate, a long slow spring
with the buds obdurate as pebbles,

too much building, so she comes to stand
in our garden, eyes flowering with wonder
under the incandescent buffet of the fruit
trees, this garden cafeteria she has walked
into to graze, from the lean late woods.

In June, the young deer are almost tame

We had met the two of them, young mates.
She was the more curious, tame.
The smell of oils and linseed drew her.
Once I saw her standing behind a painter
at the side of a sand road, looking
over his shoulder like a tourist pausing.

In the early morning we often saw them
as we did this morning. He ran across
the paved road by the dike, she
followed, and the new station wagon
driven by a doctor with Georgia plates
came roaring over the hill far too fast.

He hit her so hard she went high in the air
landed on his windshield, stumbled
forward, then lay kicking. He paused,
started away. I stood before him
flagging him down but he would not
get out. He drove off, left us with her.

I knelt by her, still thrashing,
the blood now blooming from her mouth,
running in a brilliant stream

a touch of fuchsia in the scarlet.
I had to help her die. I cradled
the beautiful head, eyes wide in terror,

I closed the windpipe with my hands.
She was bleeding so hard that
my execution was fast. Within two
minutes, she was still and her open
eye glazed over and the sweet tawny
flank was still at last.

She was the color of my Siamese Arofa
whom I had to help to die twelve
years ago. I could not let the vet
kill her. She would have known.
She could read our emotions
like captions on a foreign movie.

I think of an old man lying
in a hospital bed, his legs cut off,
his head smashed in, and the tubes
and the machines keeping him from quiet.
I have been close enough to death
to know that there is a time

when life is indistinguishable from pain,
when you want to turn your face
to the wall and pass through it
into fog that slowly lifts on the wind
and goes into the air and the earth,
each molecule becoming something else.

There is a time to be other.
But death is always irrational,
the great thing that suddenly strikes
in the middle of a morning when the locust
trees are hanging with great honeyed
bunches of sweet flowers to graze,

when every leaf is still fresh and sweet,
when the multiflora roses turn
the sand roads into bowers of perfume:
you smashed and gasping with pain,
me having to play Dr Death, pressing
your maiden throat in my shaking hands.

Burial by salt

The day after Thanksgiving I took you to the sea.
The sky was low and scudding. The wind was stiff.
The sea broke over itself in seething froth
like whipped up eggwhites, blowing to settle
in slowly popping masses at my feet.

I ran, boots on, into the bucking surf
taking you in handfuls, tossing you
into wind, into water, into the elements:
go back, give back. Time is all spent,
the flesh is spent to ashes.

Mother's were colored like a mosaic,
vivid hues of the inside of conch shells,
pastels, pearls, green, salmon as feathers
of tropical birds. They fit in my cupped hands.
I put her in the rose garden and said kaddish.

Your ashes are old movies, black into grey.
Heavy as iron filings, they sag the box
sides. They fill it to overflowing.
Handful after handful I give to the waves
which seize and churn you over and under.

I am silent as I give you to the cold
winter ocean grey as a ship of war,
the color of your eyes, grey with green
and blue washed in, that so seldom met
my gaze, that looked right through me.

What is to be said? Did you have a religion?
If so, you never spoke of it to me.
I remember you saying, *No*, saying it often
and loud, I remember you saying, *Never*,
I remember, *I won't have that in my house*.

I grew up under the threat of your anger
as peasants occupy the slopes of a volcano
sniffing the wind, repeating old adages,
reading birdflight and always waiting, even
in sleep for the ground to quake and open.

My injustices, my pains, my resentments:
they are numerous, precious as the marbles
I kept in a jar, not so much for playing
as simply rolling in my hands to see
the colors trap the light and swell.

Tossing your ashes in my hands as the waves
drag the sand from under me, trying to topple
me into the turning eddy of far storms,
I want to cast that anger from me, finally,
to say, you begot me and although my body

my hair my eyes are my mother's so that at your
funeral, your brother called me by her name,
I will agree that in the long bones of my legs,
in my knees, in my Welsh mouth that sits oddly
in my Jewish Tartar face, you are imprinted.

I was born the wrong sex to a woman
in her mid-forties who had tried to get pregnant

for five years. A hard birth,
I was her miracle and your disappointment.
Everything followed from that, downhill.

I search now through the ashes of my old pain
to find something to praise, and I find that
withholding love, you made me strive to be worthy,
reaching, always reaching, thinking that when I leaped
high enough you would be watching. You weren't.

That did not cancel the leaping or the fruit
at last grasped in the hand and gnawed to the pit.
You were the stone on which I built my strength.
Your indifference honed me. Your coldness
toughened my flesh. Your anger stropped me.

I was reading maps for family trips at age
five, navigating from the back seat. Till
I was twenty, I did not know other children
did not direct all turns and plot route numbers.
When Mother feigned helplessness, I was factotum.

Nurse, houseboy, carpenter's helper, maid,
whatever chinks appeared I filled, responsible
and rebellious with equal passion, equal time,
and thus quite primed to charge like a rocket
out the door trailing sparks at seventeen.

We were illsuited as fox and bull. Once
I stopped following baseball, we could not talk.
I'd ask you how some process was done – open
hearth steel, how generators worked.
Your answers had a clarity I savored.

I did with Mother as I had promised her,
I took her from you and brought her home to me,
I buried her as a Jew and mourn her still.

To you I made no promises. You asked none.
Forty-nine years we spoke of nothing real.

For decades I thought someday we would talk
at last. In California I came to you in the mountains
at the dam carrying that fantasy like a picnic
lunch beautifully cooked and packed, but never
to be eaten. Not by you and me.

When I think of the rare good times
I am ten or eleven and we are working together
on some task in silence. In silence I faded into
the cartoon son. Hand me the chisel. I handed.
Bevel the edge smooth. I always got bored.

I'd start asking questions, I'd start asking
why and wherefore and how come and who said so.
I was lonely on the icefield, I was lonely
in the ice caves of your sometime favor.
I kept trying to start a fire or conversation.

Time burns down and the dark rushes in in waves.
I can't lie. What was between us was history,
not love. I have striven to be just to you,
stranger, first cause, old man, my father,
and now I give you over to salt and silence.

The level

A great balance hangs in the sky
and briefly on the black pan
and on the blue pan, the melon
of the moon and the blood orange
of the sun are symmetrical
like two unmatched eyes glowing
at us with one desire.

This is an instant's equality,
a level that at once
starts to dip. In spring
the sun starts up its golden
engine earlier each dawn.
In fall, night soaks
its dye into the edges of day.

But now they hang, two bright
balls teasing us to balance
the halves of our brain, need
and will, gut and intellect,
you and me in an instant's grace –
understanding no woman, even
Gaia, can always make it work.

Morning athletes
(*for Gloria Nardin Watts*)

Most mornings we go running side by side
two women in mid-lives jogging, awkward
in our baggy improvisations, two
bundles of rejects from the thrift shop.
Men in their zippy outfits run in packs
on the road where we park, meet
like lovers on the wood's edge and walk
sedately around the corner out of sight
to our own hardened clay road, High Toss.

Slowly we shuffle, serious, panting
but talking as we trot, our old honorable
wounds in knee and back and ankle paining
us, short, fleshy, dark haired, Italian
and Jew, with our full breasts carefully
confined. We are rich earthy cooks
both of us and the flesh we are working
off was put on with grave pleasure. We
appreciate each other's cooking, each
other's art, photographer and poet, jogging
in the chill and wet and green, in the blaze
of young sun, talking over our work,
our plans, our men, our ideas, watching
each other like a pot that might boil dry
for that sign of too harsh fatigue.

It is not the running I love, thump
thump with my leaden feet that only
infrequently are winged and prancing,
but the light that glints off the cattails
as the wind furrows them, the rum cherries
reddening leaf and fruit, the way the pines

blacken the sunlight on their bristles,
the hawk circling, stooping, floating
low over beige grasses,
                              and your company
as we trot, two friendly dogs leaving
tracks in the sand. The geese call
on the river wandering lost in sedges
and we talk and pant, pant and talk
in the morning early and busy together.

For Mars and her children returning in March

1.
To name is not to possess what cannot
be owned or even known in the small words
and endless excuses of human speech.
I have adopted a Humpback Whale, Mars.

When I renew my support for whale research
a photo comes, usually her flukes –
diving or perhaps slapping the water.
Fictional bond, sucker bait, gimmick.

Last winter while humpbacks
were washing up week by week, she birthed,
the year of heaviness issuing in life,
her sisters about her attending.

So every spring I wait to see if she
returns, for naming makes valuable to us

what is unique in itself, one of four
hundred thirty-five local humpbacks we haven't yet killed.

2.
Jonah in the dark
hears the immense heart throbbing like a generator.
Tours the cathedral of the lungs.
This is the Great Kirk of Bavo
baroque organ intricate and massive as a Bach fugue
in the white ship scrubbed down to holy salt.
The air rushes in and percolates,
basalt dense as she plummets past canyons and cliffs.

Jonah sees lights dancing like those lanterns
swinging in the night the mooncussers used to hang
on horses' necks to lure ships to wreck on the great beach.
His nerves explode tracer patterns on his eyeballs.

But now above the sloshing and churning,
the engine of the heart, he hears the voice of the whale.
He is inside the organ; the lungs are its bellows.
Its pipes are fathoms tall.
He is a little cupidon cast from brass as decoration.

He is carried inside a tenor the size of a concert hall
improvising on themes he hears now from all sides,
a chamber orchestra enclosed in no chamber at all.
Clicks, squeaks, moans, trills, resonant as thunder
it sounds electronic.

In the night the tones flicker and shimmer,
fiery arias in the salty dark
nets of sound trailing through the silence
like constellations floating in the wet void.

In the cave of the whale Jonah studies
our elder brother and sister

who went down to the sea without a ship
and swam for the bottom.
Leviathan reaps the wild bounty of the wave,
without nets, without ships, without tools.
Leviathan does not slave or spend
but lashes his mighty tail and sounds
free as we never will be
and loving to his kind.

Our prayers rise like clouds of whining mosquitoes
all day and all night, give me, I want, I need,
I must have, him, her, the heart of my enemy,
a diamond as big as Leviathan,
a mountain to strip mine,
whales to harvest, while they sing
a dwindling psalm to the great eye
that watches from inside.

3.
Arcing out of the greygreen moil of water
the humpback offers her plume of praise,
steam gusting from the hot stove of her heart.

They are houses leaping,
they are oreboats upending.
Lava flows, they float on the calm.
Leather icebergs, they are sunning in the current.

Breaching, now they travel in bow curves,
viaducts, strong arches of speed,
up and over, rolling into the sea again,
huge smooth wheels turning past us.

Now she rises just beside the boat,
thrusting herself out, dark joy towering
over me where I grip the slippery wet rail.

Her steam touches my face.
Her breath enters my nose and my lungs.
That small vulnerable eye bright as a chip
of obsidian looks at me, sees me
sizes me up, small, pale, staring in awe.

We in our boats permitted among you,
spanking the waves, slamming the doors of the sea,
let us sketch our quadrille on the waves
of Stellwagen Bank where fish swirl and jump.
My shirt is wet with the breath of the whale,
an anointing, a fishy embrace.

4.
Here on this question mark of sand sprawled
gracefully on the tumbling sea,
we know the whales one by one.
In the grim harvest of last winter
the bodies washed up on the bay beaches.

A dead warbler under the leafless bayberry
may provoke us to pass by with the flash
of mourning that flesh shudders out its breath
and turns cold, fading feathers in the brown
grasses dying back. But a dead whale:
a shrieking gyre of hungry seagulls turns
and turns over the heap of it, the eye
still open and not yet picked out.
Soon it stinks like a battlefield.
The bulldozer arrives to labor at burial.

We see the little as cute, the big as impressive
although we are oftener killed by viruses
too tiny for our eye to register without
electronic aid, than by an elephant in must.

But here the loss is not impersonal, one whale

becoming the next, anonymous as rock piles in the desert.
Each is known. Beltane, Comet, Point,
Talon noted among Cape friends dead this cycle.

We must praise each humpback breaching, meet them on the
    banks,
lurch over their feeding on sand lances, herring.
Each is a poet, a composer, a scholar of the roads
below. They are always singing, and what they know
is as alien to us as if they swam past Sirius.

Naming turns the crowd into faces,
turns no man's land into someone's turf,
making a stray and starving cat a pet.
Naming makes a whale who swims through the sea
strewn with human waste and poison,
the trash of boats and cities,
the nets and shipping, known to us,
pod and matrilineal descent, travels
and fate. One community encompasses
this fragile fawn colored coil of sand
and the vast and roiling Gulf Stream river
and all of us finny, furred and feathered
who dwell in and on this living dying ocean.

If we cannot preserve the greatest of these
from our own greed, our carelessness,
then we will surely follow that shape of natural power
into the silence after its murdered song,
the sea whose hot heart has been stopped
lapping like heavy oil at beaches
where only plastic shards cast up on the stained sand.

STREET SMARTS

Joy Road and Livernois

My name was Pat. We used to read Poe in bed
till we heard blood dripping in the closet.
I fell in love with a woman who could ring
all bells of my bones tolling, jangling.
But she in her cape and her Caddy
had to shine in the eyes of the other pimps,
a man among monkeys, so she turned me on the streets
to strut my meek ass. To quiet my wailing
she taught me to slip the fire in my arm,
the white thunder rolling over till nothing
hurt but coming down. One day I didn't.
I was fifteen. My face gleamed in the casket.

My name was Evie. We used to shoplift,
my giggling, wide-eyed questions, your fast hands;
we picked up boys together on the corners.
The cops busted me for stealing, milled me,
sent me up for prostitution because I weren't
no virgin. I met my boyfriend in the courts.
Together we robbed a liquor store that wouldn't
sell us whiskey. I liked to tote a gun.
It was the cleanest thing I ever held.
It was the only power I ever had.
I could look any creep straight on in the eyes.
A state trooper blew my face off in Marquette.

My name was Peggy. Across the street from the gas-
works, my mom raised nine kids. My brother-
in-law porked me while my sister gave birth
choking me with the pillow when I screamed.
I got used to it. My third boyfriend knocked me up.
Now I've been pregnant for twenty years,
always a belly bigger than me to push around

like a overloaded wheelbarrow ready to spill
on the blacktop. Now it's my last one,
a tumor big as a baby when they found it.
When I look in the mirror I see my mom.
Remember how we braided each other's hair,
mine red, yours black. Now I'm bald
as a egg and nearly boiled through.

I was Teresa. I used to carry a long clasp
knife I stole from my uncle. Running nights
through the twitching streets, I'd finger it.
It made me feel as mean as any man.
My boyfriend worked on cars until they flew.
All those hot nights riding around and around
when we had no place to go but back.
Those chrome nights we raced out on the highway
faster faster till the blood fizzed in my throat
like shaken soda. It shot in an arc
when he hit the pole and I went out the windshield,
the knife I showed you how to use, still
on its leather thong between my breasts
where it didn't save me from being cut in two.

I was Gladys. Like you, I stayed in school.
I did not lay down in back seats with boys.
I became a nurse, married, had three sons.
My ankles swelled. I worked the night hours
among the dying and accident cases. My husband
left me for a girl he met in a bar, left debts,
a five-year-old Chevy, a mortgage.
My oldest came home in a body bag. My youngest
ran off. The middle one drinks beer and watches
the soaps since the Kelsey-Hayes plant closed.
Then my boy began to call me from the alley.
Every night he was out there calling, Mama,
help me! It hurts, Mama! Take me home.

This is the locked ward and the drugs
eat out my head like busy worms.

With each of them I lay down, my twelve-
year-old scrawny tough body like weathered
wood pressed to their pain, and we taught
each other love and pleasure and ourselves.
We invented the places, the sounds, the smells,
the little names. At twelve I was violent
in love, a fiery rat, a whip snake,
a starving weasel, all teeth and speed
except for the sore fruit of my new breasts
pushing out. What did I learn? To value
my pleasure and how little the love of women
can shield against the acid city rain.

You surge among my many ghosts. I never think
I got out because I was smart, brave, hardworking, attractive. Evie was brave.
Gladys and Teresa were smart. Peggy worked
sixteen hours. Pat gleamed like olivewood
polished to a burnish as if fire lived in wood.
I wriggled through an opening left just big enough
for one. There is no virtue in survival
only luck, and a streak of indifference
that I could take off and keep going.

I got out of those Detroit blocks where the air
eats stone and melts flesh, where jobs
dangle and you jump and jump, where there are
more drugs than books, more ways to die
than ways to live, because I ran fast,
ran hard, and never stopped looking back.
It is not looking back that turned me
to salt, no, I taste my salt from the mines
under Detroit, the salt of our common juices.
Girls who lacked everything except trouble,

contempt and rough times, girls
used like urinals, you are the salt
keeps me from rotting as the years swell.
I am the fast train you are traveling in
to a world of a different color, and the love
we cupped so clumsily in our hands to catch
rages and drives onward, an engine of light.

The cats of Greece

The cats of Greece have
eyes grey as plague.
Their voices are limpid,
all hunger.
As they dodge in the gutters
their bones clack.
Dogs run from them.
In tavernas they sit
at tableside and
watch you eat.
Their moonpale cries
hurl themselves
against your full spoon.
If you touch one gently
it goes crazy.
Its eyes turn up.
It wraps itself
around your ankle
and purrs a rusty millennium,
you liar,
you tourist.

Rape poem

There is no difference between being raped
and being pushed down a flight of cement steps
except that the wounds also bleed inside.

There is no difference between being raped
and being run over by a truck
except that afterward men ask if you enjoyed it.

There is no difference between being raped
and being bit on the ankle by a rattlesnake
except that people ask if your skirt was short
and why you were out alone anyhow.

There is no difference between being raped
and going head first through a windshield
except that afterward you are afraid
not of cars
but half the human race.

The rapist is your boyfriend's brother.
He sits beside you in the movies eating popcorn.
Rape fattens on the fantasies of the normal male
like a maggot in garbage.

Fear of rape is a cold wind blowing
all of the time on a woman's hunched back.
Never to stroll alone on a sand road through pine woods,
never to climb a trail across a bald
without that aluminum in the mouth
when I see a man climbing toward me.

Never to open the door to a knock
without that razor just grazing the throat.
The fear of the dark side of hedges,

the back seat of the car, the empty house
rattling keys like a snake's warning.
The fear of the smiling man
in whose pocket is a knife.
The fear of the serious man
in whose fist is locked hatred.

All it takes to cast a rapist is seeing your body
as jackhammer, as blowtorch, as adding-machine-gun.
All it takes is hating that body
your own, your self, your muscle that softens to flab.

All it takes is to push what you hate,
what you fear onto the soft alien flesh.
To bucket out invincible as a tank
armored with treads without senses
to possess and punish in one act,
to rip up pleasure, to murder those who dare
live in the leafy flesh open to love.

Half past home

Morning rattles the tall spike fence.
Already the old are set out to get dirty in the sun
spread like drying coverlets around the garden
by straggly hedges smelling of tomcat.
From the steep oxblood hospital
hunched under its miser's frown of roof,
dishes mutter, pumps work, an odor
of disinfectant slops into the street
toward the greygreen quadrangles of the university.
Pickets with the facts of their poverty hoisted on sticks
turn in the street like a tattered washing.

The trustees decline to negotiate
for this is a charitable institution.

Among the houses of the poor and black nearby
a crane nods waist-high among broken bedrooms.
Already the university digs foundations
to be hallowed with the names of trustees.
The dish and bottle washers, the orderlies march
carrying the crooked sick toward death on their backs.
The neighborhood is being cured of poverty.
Busses will carry the mop pushers in and out.

Are the old dying too slowly in their garden?
Under elms spacious and dusty
as roominghouse porches the old men mutter
that they are closing the north wing,
for the land is valuable when you get down to it,
and they will, down to the prairie dog bones.
This is the Home for Incurables, and the old are,
like the blindness of trustees.
The hoarse wind blows, mile after mile
while Chicago smokes sweetly as a barbecue
and sizzles like acid under nobody's sun.

A work of artifice

The bonsai tree
in the attractive pot
could have grown eighty feet tall
on the side of a mountain
till split by lightning
but a gardener

carefully pruned it.
It is nine inches high.
Every day as he
whittles back the branches
the gardener croons,
it is your nature
to be small and cozy,
domestic and weak:
how lucky, little tree,
to have a pot to grow in.
With living creatures
one must begin very early
to dwarf their growth:
the bound feet,
the crippled brain,
the hair in curlers,
the hands you
love to touch.

Phyllis wounded

To fight history as it carries us,
to swim upstream across the currents – no! –
to move the river, to create new currents
with the force of our arms and backs,
to shape this torrent as it shapes us
flowing, churning, dragging us under
into the green moil where the breath is pummeled
from the lungs and the eyes burst backward,
among rocks, the teeth of the white water
grinning like hungry bears:
ah, Phyllis, you complain too much!

[132]

We all carry in gold lockets
of the good birthday child sentimental
landscapes in pale mauve where we have
everything we desire carried in on trays.
We are serene as jade buddhas,
respectable as Jane Austen,
secure as an obituary in *The Times*.

We were not made for a heaven of Sundays.
Most people are given hunger, the dim pain
of being used twisting through the bowels,
close walls and a low sky, troubles visited
from above like tornadoes that level the house,
pain early, pain late and a death not chosen.

My friend, the amazons were hideous
with the white scars of knife wounds,
the welts of sword slashes, flesh that would
remind nobody of a ripe peach.
But age sucks us all dry.

Old campaigners waken to the resonant singing
of angels of fire and newsprint
who only trouble the sleep of women
who climb on a platform or crouch at a barricade.
Your smile is rich with risk
and subtle with enemies contested.
Your memories whistle and clang and moan
in the dark like buoys that summon
and give warning of danger
and the channel through.

I was not born a serf bound to a ryefield,
I was not born to bend over a pressing machine
in a loft while the sun rose and set, I was not born
to starve in the first year with big
belly and spindly legs, I was not born

to be gang raped by soldiers at fourteen,
I was not born to die in childbirth,
to be burned at the stake by the Church,
but of all these we are the daughters
born of luck round as an apple
and fat as a goose, to charge into battle
swinging our great-grandmothers' bones.
Millions of dead women keen in our hair
for food and freedom. The electricity
drives me humming. What privilege
to be the heiresses of so much wanting!
How can we ever give up?

Our laughter has been honed by adversity
till it gleams like an ax
and we will not die by our own hand.

The market economy

Suppose some peddler offered
you can have a color TV
but your baby will be
born with a crooked spine;
you can have wash and wear
suits but it will cost
you your left lung
rotted with cancer; suppose
somebody offered you
a frozen precooked dinner
every night for ten years
but at the end
your colon dies

and then you do,
slowly and with much pain.
You get a house in the suburbs
but you work in a new plastics
factory and die at fifty-one
when your kidneys turn off.

But where else will you
work? Where else can
you rent but Smog City?
The only houses you can afford
are under the yellow sky.
You've been out of work for
a year and they're hiring
at the plastics factory.
Don't read the fine
print, there isn't any.

The butt of winter

The city lies grey and sopping like a dead rat
under the slow oily rain.
Between the Lower East Side tenements
the sky is a snotty handkerchief.
The garbage of poor lives slimes the streets.
You lie on your bed and think
soon it will be hot and violent,
then it will be cold and mean.
You say you feel as empty
as a popbottle in the street.
You say you feel full of cold water

standing like an old horse trough.
The clock ticks, somewhat wrong.
The walls crack their dry knuckles.
Work is only other rooms where people cough,
only the typewriter clucking like a wrong clock.

Nobody will turn the soiled water into wine,
nobody will shout cold Lazarus alive
but you. You are your own magician.
Stretch out your hand,
stretch out your hand and look:
each finger is a snake of energy,
a gaggle of craning necks.
Each electric finger conducts the world.
Each finger is a bud's eye opening.
Each finger is a vulnerable weapon.
The sun is floating in your belly like a fish.
Light creaks in your bones.
You are sleeping with your tail in your mouth.
Unclench your hands and look.
Nothing is given us but each other.
We have nothing to give
but ourselves.
We have nothing to take but the time
that drips, drips anyhow
leaving a brown stain.
Open your eyes and your belly.
Let the sun rise into your chest and burn your throat,
stretch out your hands and tear the gauzy rain
that your world can be born from you
screaming and red.

The root canal

You see before you an icing of skin,
a scum of flesh
narrowly wrapped around a tooth.
This tooth is red as a lion's
heart and it throbs.
This tooth is hollowed out to a cave
big enough for tourists
to go through in parties with guides
in flat-bottomed boats.
This tooth sings opera all night
like a Russian basso profundo.
This tooth plays itself like an organ
in an old movie palace; it is
the chief villain, Sydney Greenstreet,
and its laughter tickles with menace.
This tooth is dying, dying
like a cruel pharaoh, like a fat
gouty old tyrant assembling
his wives and his cabinet, his horse
and his generals, his dancing girls
and his hunting cheetah, all
to be burned on his tomb
in homage. I am nothing,
nothing at all, but a reluctant
pyramid standing here, a grandiose
talking headstone for my tooth.

If they come in the night

Long ago on a night of danger and vigil
a friend said, *Why are you happy?*
He explained (we lay together
on a hard cold floor) what prison
meant because he had done
time, and I talked of the death
of friends. *Why are you happy
then*, he asked, close to
angry.

I said, I like my life. If I
have to give it back, if they
take it from me, let me only
not feel I wasted any, let me
not feel I forgot to love anyone
I meant to love, that I forgot
to give what I held in my hands,
that I forgot to do some little
piece of the work that wanted
to come through.

Sun and moonshine, starshine,
the muted grey light off the waters
of the bay at night, the white
light of the fog stealing in,
the first spears of the morning
touching a face
I love. We all lose
everything. We lose
ourselves. We are lost.

Only what we manage to do
lasts, what love sculpts from us;
but what I count, my rubies, my

children, are those moments
wide open when I know clearly
who I am, who you are, what we
do, a marigold, an oakleaf, a meteor,
with all my senses hungry and filled
at once like a pitcher with light.

The long death
(*for Wendy Teresa Simon 1954–1979*)

Radiation is like oppression
the average daily kind of subliminal toothache
you get almost used to, the stench
of chlorine in the water, of smog in the wind.

We comprehend the disasters of the moment,
the nursing home fire, the river in flood
pouring through the sand bag levee, the airplane
crash with fragments of burnt bodies
scattered among the hunks of twisted metal.

But how to grasp a thing that does not
kill you today or tomorrow
but slowly from the inside in twenty years.
How to feel that a corporate choice
means we bear twisted genes and our
grandchildren will be stillborn if our
children are very lucky.

Slow death can not be photographed for the six
o'clock news. It's all statistical,
the gross national product or the prime
lending rate. Yet if our eyes saw

in the right spectrum, how it would shine,
lurid as magenta neon.

If we could smell radiation like seeping
gas, if we could sense it as heat, if we
could hear it as a low ominous roar
of the earth shifting, then we would not sit
and be poisoned while industry spokesmen
talk of acceptable millirems
and cancer per population thousand.

We acquiesce at murder so long as it is slow,
murder from asbestos dust, from tobacco,
from lead in the water, from sulfur in the air,
and fourteen years later statistics are printed
on the rise in leukemia among children.
We never see their faces. They never stand,
those poisoned children together in a courtyard,
and are gunned down by men in three-piece suits.

The soft spring rain floats down and the air
is perfumed with pine and earth. Seedlings
drink it in, robins sip it in puddles,
you run in it and feel clean and strong,
the spring rain blowing from the irradiated
cloud over the power plant.

Radiation is oppression, the daily average
kind, the kind you're almost used to
and live with as the years abrade you,
high blood pressure, ulcers, cramps, migraine,
a hacking cough: you take it inside
and it becomes pain and you say, not
They are killing me, but *I am sick now*.

More that winter ends than spring begins

Nothing stirs out of the earth,
yet the dogs are trotting in odd
pairs of greyhound and spaniel;
in small packs with brisk intent
they cross the streets. All over
Cambridge you can hear them barking,
sniffing each other in greeting,
raising their muzzles to drink the air.
Lust turns them daffy and grim.

Pigeons too are strutting on roof
trees like animate sofa pillows,
puffing and cooing as they court
in the storm gutters. The old cat
crouching wary on the stoop suddenly
turns on her back and squirming
white belly up, rolls on sun heated
concrete with a sensuous shudder.

The low road

What can they do
to you? Whatever they want.
They can set you up, they can
bust you, they can break
your fingers, they can
burn your brain with electricity,
blur you with drugs till you
can't walk, can't remember; they can
take your child, wall up
your lover. They can do anything
you can't stop them
from doing. How can you stop
them? Alone, you can fight,
you can refuse, you can
take what revenge you find
but they roll over you.

But two people fighting
back to back can cut through
a mob, a snake-dancing file
can break a cordon, an army
can meet an army.

Two people can keep each other
sane, can give support, conviction,
love, massage, hope, sex.
Three people are a delegation,
a committee, a wedge. With four
you can play bridge and start
an organization. With six
you can rent a whole house,
eat pie for dinner with no
seconds and hold a fund raising party.

A dozen make a demonstration.
A hundred fill a hall.
A thousand have solidarity and your own newsletter;
ten thousand, visibility and your own paper;
a hundred thousand, your own media;
ten million, your own country.

It goes on one at a time.
It starts when you care
to act, it starts when you do
it again after they said no.
It starts when you say *We*
and know who you mean, and each
day you mean one more.

For strong women

A strong woman is a woman who is straining.
A strong woman is a woman standing
on tiptoe and lifting a barbell
while trying to sing *Boris Godunov*.
A strong woman is a woman at work
cleaning out the cesspool of the ages
and while she shovels, she talks about
how she doesn't mind crying, it opens
the ducts of the eyes, and throwing up
develops the stomach muscles, and
she goes on shoveling with tears
in her nose.

A strong woman is a woman in whose head
a voice is repeating, I told you so,

ugly, bad girl, bitch, nag, shrill, witch,
ballbuster, nobody will ever love you back,
why aren't you feminine, why aren't
you soft, why aren't you quiet, why
aren't you dead?

A strong woman is a woman determined
to do something others are determined
not be done. She is pushing up on the bottom
of a lead coffin lid. She is trying to raise
a manhole cover with her head, she is trying
to butt her way through a steel wall.
Her head hurts. People waiting for the hole
to be made say, Hurry, you're so strong.

A strong woman is a woman bleeding
inside. A strong woman is a woman making
herself strong every morning while her teeth
loosen and her back throbs. Every baby,
a tooth, midwives used to say, and now
every battle a scar. A strong woman
is a mass of scar tissue that aches
when it rains and wounds that bleed
when you bump them and memories that get up
in the night and clump in boots to and fro.

A strong woman is a woman who craves love
like oxygen or she turns blue choking.
A strong woman is a woman who loves
strongly and weeps strongly and is strongly
terrified and has strong needs. She is strong
in words, in action, in connection, in feeling;
she is not strong as a stone but as a wolf
suckling her young. Strength is not in her
but she enacts it as a wind fills a sail.

What comforts her is others loving
her equally for the strength and for the weakness
from which it issues, lightning from a cloud.
Lightning stuns. In rain, the clouds disperse.
Only water of connection remains,
flowing through us. Strong is what we make
each other. Until we are all strong together,
a strong woman is a woman strongly afraid.

Pop-sicle

Martina had a mama, Anna-Lisa
and a papa and a house on the corner
of the block with a birch tree
and Herbie the Hamster.
Herbie let her carry him in her blouse
and never bit her, although
his claws were pins sticking her.

When her papa yelled, Herbie would
wake too and scrabble in his cage.
His beady eyes looked at her without
a moment's anger and never swelled
with tears like her mama's.
Papa would pull on her and
then Mama would pull on her.

Then Mama took her to Grandma.
A week after they moved into
Mama's old room, Herbie died.
Mama put him in a box

in the freezer till the ground thawed.
Mama got a job in a doctor's office.
They moved to a yellow brick building.

Anna-Lisa got sick and lost the job.
They lived with Mama's boyfriend
Carl and then back to sour Grandma
and then to a new boyfriend Jerry.
Herbie goes along in his box.
Spring has come and gone
four times, but Martina will

not give Herbie to the embrace
of somebody else's earth. He is
her lost love, her cropped roots
as they move from one man's apartment
to another man's house. They are not
fathers. Martina glares at the men from
slitted eyes. Herbie's still frozen.

They inhabit me

I am pregnant with certain deaths
of women who choked before they could speak
could speak their names
could know their names
before they had names to know.

I am owl, the spirit said,
I swim through the darkness on wide wings.
I see what is behind me
as well as what is before.
In the morning a splash of blood

on the snow marks where I found
what I needed. In the mild
light of day the crows mob
me cursing. Are you the daughter
of my amber clocktower eyes?

I am pregnant with certain deaths
of women whose hands were replaced
by paper flowers, which must be kept
clean, which could tear on a glance,
which could not hold even water.

I am cat. I rub your prejudices
against the comfortable way they grow.
I am fastidious, not as a careful
housewife, but as a careful lover,
keeping genitals as clean as face.

I turn up my belly of warm sensuality
to your fingers, purring my pleasure
and letting my claws just tip out.
Are you the daughter of the fierce
aria of my passion scrawled on the night?

I am pregnant with certain deaths
of women who dreamed that the lover
would strike like lightning and throw
them over the crupper and carry them off.
It was the ambulance that came.

I am wolf. I call across the miles
my messages of yearning and hunger,
and the snow speaks to me constantly
of food and want and friend and foe.
The iron air is heavy with ice

tweaking my nose and the sound
of the wind is sharp and whetted.
Commenting, chatting, calling

we run through the net of scents
querying, are you my daughter?

I am pregnant with deaths of certain
women who curled wound in the skeins
of dream, who secreted silk
from spittle and bound themselves
in swaddling clothes of shrouds.

I am raccoon. I thrive in woods,
I thrive in the alleys of your cities.
With my little hands I open
whatever you shut away from me.
On your garbage I grow glossy.

Among packs of stray dogs I bare
my teeth, and the warring rats part.
I flourish like the ailanthus tree;
in your trashheaps I dig underground
castles. Are you my daughter?

I am pregnant with certain deaths
of women who wander slamming doors
and sighing as if to be overheard,
talking to themselves like water left
running, tears dried to table salt.

They hide in my hair like crabs,
they are banging on the nodes of my spine
as on the door of a tardy elevator.
They want to ride up to the observation
platform and peer out my eyes for the view.

All this wanting creates a black hole
where ghosts and totems whirl and join
passing through into antimatter of art,
the alternate universe in which such certain
deaths as theirs and mine throb with light.

The three of cups
(*from the sequence 'Laying Down the Tower', based on the Tarot*)

A poem is a dancing. It goes out of a mouth to your ears
and for some moments aligns us
so we wheel and turn together.
The blackbirds dance over the marsh as they drive off the hawk.
The marsh hawks hunt in spirals paired, crying.
The bees dance where the pollen is to be gathered
and dance their fierce mating.

When I dance I forget myself, I am danced.
Music fills me to overflowing and the power moves
up from my feet to my fingers, making leaves as sap does.

My dance is of you: we are dancing together though scattered,
atomistic as Brownian motes, the same music holds us.
Even after we have discovered we are death's darling children
born of the print-out, the laser, the war-game
we still must bear joy back into the world.
We must shake off the oil of passivity and no more be spectators
even before the masque of our own dark and bright dreams.

We grew up in Disneyland with ads for friends
and believed we could be made new by taking a pill.
We wanted instant revolution, where all we had to add
was a little smoke.
We shall survive only if we win; they will kill us
if they can, and killing is what they do best.
We have learned to do nothing well.
We are still strangers to our bodies,
tools fit awkwardly in our hands, our weapons explode,
we speak to each other haltingly in phrases they gave us.

Taste what is in your mouth;
if it is water, still taste it.
Wash out the cups of your fingers,

clean your eyes with new tears for your sister.
We are not less political if we remember
that the universe itself pulses like a heart;
that the blood dances with us; that joy is a power
treading with hooves and talons on our flimsy bodies;
that water flows and fire leaps and the land gives strength
if you build on it with respect, if you dance on it with vigor,
if you put seeds in with care and give back what is left over;
that a ritual of unity makes some of what it pretends;
that every thing is part of something else.

SHOULDER TO THE WHEEL

To be of use

The people I love the best
jump into work head first
without dallying in the shallows
and swim off with sure strokes almost out of sight.
They seem to become natives of that element,
the black sleek heads of seals
bouncing like half-submerged balls.

I love people who harness themselves, an ox to a heavy cart,
who pull like water buffalo, with massive patience,
who strain in the mud and the muck to move things forward,
who do what has to be done, again and again.

I want to be with people who submerge
in the task, who go into the fields to harvest
and work in a row and pass the bags along,
who are not parlor generals and field deserters
but move in a common rhythm
when the food must come in or the fire be put out.

The work of the world is common as mud.
Botched, it smears the hands, crumbles to dust.
But the thing worth doing well done
has a shape that satisfies, clean and evident.
Greek amphoras for wine or oil,
Hopi vases that held corn, are put in museums
but you know they were made to be used.
The pitcher cries for water to carry
and a person for work that is real.

The morning half-life blues

Girls buck the wind in the grooves toward work
in fuzzy coats promised to be warm as fur.
The shop windows snicker
flashing them hurrying over dresses they cannot afford:
you are not pretty enough, not pretty enough.

Blown with yesterday's papers through the boiled coffee
    morning
they dream of the stop on the subway without a name,
the door in the heart of the grove of skyscrapers,
that garden where we nestle to the teats of a furry world,
lie in mounds of peony eating grapes,
and need barter ourselves for nothing,
not by the hour, not by the pound, not by the skinful,
that party to which no one will give or sell us the key
though we have all thought briefly we had found it
drunk or in bed.

Black girls with thin legs and high necks stalking like herons,
plump girls with blue legs and green eyelids and strawberry
    breasts,
swept off to be frozen in fluorescent cubes,
the vacuum of your jobs sucks your brains dry
and fills you with the ooze of melted comics.
Living is later. This is your rented death.
You grasp at brand commodities and vague lusts
to make up, to pay for each day
which opens like a can and is empty, and then another,
afternoons like dinosaur eggs stuffed with glue.

Girls of the dirty morning, ticketed and spent,
you will be less at forty than at twenty.
Your living is a waste product of somebody's mill.

I would fix you like buds to a city where people work
to make and do things necessary and good,
where work is real as bread and babies and trees in parks
and you would blossom slowly and ripen to sound fruit.

The woman in the ordinary

The woman in the ordinary pudgy downcast girl
is crouching with eyes and muscles clenched.
Round and pebble smooth she effaces herself
under ripples of conversation and debate.
The woman in the block of ivory soap
has massive thighs that neigh,
great breasts that blare and strong arms that trumpet.
The woman of the golden fleece
laughs uproariously from the belly
inside the girl who imitates
a Christmas card virgin with glued hands,
who fishes for herself in others' eyes,
who stoops and creeps to make herself smaller.
In her bottled up is a woman peppery as curry,
a yam of a woman of butter and brass,
compounded of acid and sweet like a pineapple,
like a handgrenade set to explode,
like goldenrod ready to bloom.

The bumpity road to mutual devotion

Do you remember the first raw winter
of our women's group, both of us fierce as mother bears?
Every day came down like a pile driver in the morning
shaking the bed empty
stomping sleep like a run over bag.
Our pain was new, a too sharp kitchen knife.
We bled on everything we touched.
I could hardly type for scars.
Rage sang like a coloratura doing trills
in my head as I ricocheted up male streets.
You came on like a sergeant of marines.
You were freshly ashamed of your beauty
believing if you frowned a lot no one
would notice your face.
The group defined us the strong ones,
loved us, hated us, baited us, set us
one on the other. We met
almost clandestinely. You brought flowers.
We praised lesbian love intellectually, looking
hard in each other's black eyes, and each stayed
on her side of the kitchen exuding
a nervous whine like an avalanche of white mice.

What a rutted road through thick gassy clouds of nightmare,
political bedlam. Each has let
the other down and picked her up.
We will never be lovers; too scared
of losing each other. What tantalizes past flesh
– too mirrored, lush, dark haired and soft in the belly –
is the strange mind rasping, clanging, engaging.
What we fantasize – rising like a bird kite
on the hot afternoon air – is work together.

Projects, battles, schemes, manifestos
are born from the brushing of wills
like small sparks from loose hair,
and will we let them fade, static electricity?

What shall we do before
they crush us? How far will we travel
to no country on earth?
What houses should we build? and which tear down?
what chapels, what bridges, what power stations
and stations of that burning green energy
beyond the destruction of power?
Trust me with your hand. For us to be friends
is a mating of eagle and ostrich, from both sides.

The death of the small commune

The death of the small commune
is almost accomplished.
I find it hard now to believe
in connection beyond the couple,
hard as broken bone.
Time for withdrawal and healing.
Time for lonely work
spun out of the torn gut.
Time for touching turned up earth,
for trickling seed from the palm,
thinning the shoots of green herb.
What we wanted to build
was a way station for journeying
to a new world,
but we could not agree long enough
to build the second wall,

could not love long enough
to move the heavy stone on stone,
not listen with patience
to make a good plan,
we could not agree.
Nothing remains but a shallow hole,
nothing remains
but a hole
in everything.

Song of the fucked duck

In using there are always two.
The manipulator dances with a partner who cons herself.
There are lies that glow so brightly we consent
to give a finger and then an arm
to let them burn.
I was dazzled by the crowd where everyone called my name.
Now I stand outside the funhouse exit, down the slide
reading my guidebook of Marx in Esperanto
and if I don't know anymore which way means forward
down is where my head is, next to my feet.
Form follows function, says the organizer
and turns himself into a paper clip,
into a vacuum cleaner,
into a machine gun.
Function follows analysis
but the forebrain
is only an owl in the tree of self.
One third of life we prowl in the grottoes of sleep
where neglected worms ripen into dragons,
where the spoiled pencil swells into an oak,

and the cows of our early sins are called home chewing their cuds
and turning the sad faces of our childhood upon us.
Come back and scrub the floor, the stain is still there,
come back with your brush and kneel down,
scrub and scrub again, it will never be clean.
Buried desires sprout like mushrooms on the chin of the morning.
The will to be totally rational
is the will to be made out of glass and steel:
and to use others as if they were glass and steel.
We trust with our hands and our mouths.
The cunt accepts. The teeth and back reject.
What we have to give each other:
dumb and mysterious as water swirling.
Always in the long corridors of the psyche
doors are opening and doors are slamming shut.
We rise each day to give birth or to murder
selves that go through our hands like tiny fish.
You said: I am the organizer and took and used.
You wrapped your head in theory's yards of gauze
and touched others only as tools that fit to your task.
Arrogance is not a revolutionary virtue.
The mad bulldozers of ego level the ground.
I was a tool that screamed in the hand.
I have been loving you so long and hard and mean
and the taste of you is part of my tongue
and your face is burnt into my eyelids
and I could build you with my fingers out of dust.
Now it is over. Whether we want or not
our roots go down to strange waters,
we are creatures of the seasons and the earth.
You always had a reason and you have them still
rattling like dry leaves on a stunted tree.

In the men's room(s)

When I was young I believed in intellectual conversation:
I thought the patterns we wove on stale smoke
floated off to the heaven of ideas.
To be certified worthy of high masculine discourse
like a potato on a grater I would rub on contempt,
suck snubs, wade proudly through the brown stuff on the floor.
They were talking of integrity and existential ennui
while the women ran out for six-packs and had abortions
in the kitchen and fed the children and were auctioned off.

Eventually of course I learned how their eyes perceived me:
when I bore to them cupped in my hands a new poem to nibble,
when I brought my aerial maps of Sartre or Marx,
they said, she is trying to attract our attention,
she is offering up her breasts and thighs.
I walked on eggs, their tremulous equal:
they saw a fish peddler hawking in the street.

Now I get coarse when the abstract nouns start flashing.
I go out to the kitchen to talk cabbages and habits.
I try hard to remember to watch what people do.
Yes, keep your eyes on the hands, let the voice go buzzing.
Economy is the bone, politics is the flesh,
watch who they beat and who they eat,
watch who they relieve themselves on, watch who they own.
The rest is decoration.

Report of the Fourteenth Subcommittee on Convening a Discussion Group

This is how things begin to tilt into change,
how coalitions are knit from strands of hair,
of barbed wire, twine, knitting wool and gut,
how people ease into action arguing each inch,
but the tedium of it is watching granite erode.

Let us meet to debate meeting, the day, the time,
the length. Let us discuss whether we will sit
or stand or hang from the ceiling or take it lying
down. Let us argue about the chair and the table and
the chairperson and the motion to table the chair.

In the room fog gathers under the ceiling and thickens
in every brain. Let us form committees spawning
subcommittees all laying little moldy eggs of reports.
Under the grey fluorescent sun they will crack
to hatch scuttling lizards of more committees.

The Pliocene gathers momentum and fades.
The earth tilts on its axis. More and more snows
fall each winter and less melt each spring.
A new ice age is pressing the glaciers forward
over the floor. We watch the wall of ice advance.

We are evolving into mollusks, barnacles
clinging to wood and plastic, metal and smoke
while the stale flotsam laden tide of rhetoric
inches up the shingle and dawdles back.
This is true virtue: to sit here and stay awake,

to listen, to argue, to wade on through the muck
wrestling to some momentary small agreement

like a pinhead pearl prized from a dragon-oyster.
I believe in this democracy as I believe
there is blood in my veins, but oh, oh, in me

lurks a tyrant with a double-bladed ax who longs
to swing it wide and shining, who longs to stand
and shriek, You Shall Do as I Say, pig-bastards.
No more committees but only picnics and orgies
and dances. I have spoken. So be it forevermore.

Absolute zero in the brain

Penfield the great doctor did a lobotomy
on his own sister and recorded
pages of clinical observations
on her lack of initiative afterward.

Dullness, he wrote, is superseded
by euphoria at times. Slight hemi-
paresis with aphasia. The rebellious sister
died from the head down into the pages

of medical journals and Penfield founded
a new specialty. Intellectuals
sneer at moviegoers who confuse
Dr Frankenstein with his monster.

The fans think Frankenstein is the monster.
Isn't he?

True romance

In a room with a nylon carpet and a daybed
a woman is dancing with her eyes on the TV set.
The face of the singer gluts. For her
he is singing, this face more familiar
than any lover's, this man she has carried
wrapped like a chocolate in the crisp paper
of her heart since she was fifteen.

She loves him, she loves him, for him
she dances, thrusting her hips, arms reaching,
churning her mons at his face bigger than
the face of her husband and closer,
more real than the smell of her own sweat.

O sunbright hero whose strut is paid for
by Japanese cars, by computers, by lite beer.
O lithe bodies the camera fills with buttercream
of wishes, bodies thin and flawless as blank paper,
bodies with nipples and navels taped, bodies
on which the clothes are glued, faces coated
with polyurethane, how many men paw at their
wives' flesh trying to unearth your vinyl.

Things move fast in that bright world. A man
sees a woman across a room and she smiles
only at him. After a diet soda commercial,
she is in bed with him. In the next scene
she is gone and his buddy the talking dog
goes at his side. Then the cars chase each other
off cliffs into balls of flame. The hero
steps out with a grin promising he will unzip
you, walk into the set of your head, turn up
the brightness and volume control till you
become real too, as the box glued to your eyes.

Excursions, incursions

1.

'Learning to manage the process
of technological innovation
more productively' is the theme
of the speech the man beside me
on the plane to Washington
will be saying to a Congressional
subcommittee. He works at M.I.T.
He drinks a martini, glancing sideways.
His watch flashes numbers; it houses
a tiny computer. He observes
me in snatches, data to analyze:
the two-piece V-neck dress
from New York, the manuscript
I am cutting, the wild black
hair, the dirt under my stubby nails.
It doesn't scan. I pretend
I do not see him looking
while I try to read his speech,
pretending not to: a neutron
bomb of deadly language that kills
all warm-blooded creatures
but leaves the system standing.
He rates my face and body attractive but the presence
disturbing. I try to decide
if I can learn anything useful
to my side if I let him
engage me in a game of
conversation.

2.

At the big round table in the university
club, the faculty are chatting
about wives, marriages, divorces, visiting
arrangements. They all belong
to the same kinship system. They have
one partner at a time, then terminate.
Monogamy means that the husband has
sex only a couple of times with each
other female, I figure out, and
the wife, only with him. Afterwards
the children spend summers/weekends/
Sundays with the father.

Listening becomes eavesdropping and they
begin to feel my silence like a horse
in the diningroom. Gradually as I sit
my hair mats. Feathers stick up from
it, crow and eagle. My cheeks break
out into painted zigzag designs. My spear
leans against the back of my chair.
They begin to question me, oh, um,
do you live communally? What do
you mean, 'open'? Hair breaks through
the back of my hands. My fangs
drum on the table top. In another moment
I will swing by my long prehensile
tail from the crystal chandelier,
shitting in the soup.

3.

The men are laughing as I approach
and then they price me: that calculating
scan. Everything turns into hornets

buzzing, swarming. One will
tell me about his wife
weeping tears of pure beersuds;
one is even now swaggering down
the Tombstone set of his mind, the fastest
gun; one will let me know in the next
half hour he thinks political writers
are opportunistic simpletons, and women
have minds of goat fudge; one will
only try unceasingly to bed me as if
I were the week's prize, and he wears
a chain of fellowships and grants
like sharpshooters' medals. Mostly they
will chase the students and drink, mostly
they will gossip and put each other
down, mostly they will complain. I
am here for the women, a political
task. They think they have a label
for that. I am on vacation from sex
and love, from the fatty broth
of my life. I am seeking to be useful,
the good godmother. We are acting
in different fables. I know the plots
of theirs, but none of them recognize
mine, except the students, who understand
at once they will be allowed
to chew me to the bones.

4.
I am sitting on a kitchen chair.
My feet do not reach the floor.
If I sit forward, they'll rest on
a rung, but if I do that, the women
will stop talking and look at me
and I'll be made to go outside

and 'play' in this taffeta dress.
What they say is not what they
are talking about, which lumps
just underneath. If I listen, if I
screw up my face and hold my breath
and listen, I'll see it, the moving
bump under the rug, that snake in the
tablecloth jungle, the bulge
in women's dresses you aren't supposed
to notice. I listen and listen
but it doesn't go anyplace.
I kick the table leg and am sent
outside to sulk, still not knowing.

I never got there, into the hot
wet heart of the kitchen gossip,
to sit twisting the ring worn smooth
on my finger, saying my hubby, my old
man, *him*. I never grew up, Mama
I grew off, I grew outside. I grew
like crazy. I am the calico
mouse gnawing at the foundations.
The sweet snake is my friend who chews
on the roots of the hangman's tree
to bring it down. I am the lump
under the tablecloth that moves
stealthily toward the cream pitcher.
After years under the rug like a tumor
they invite me into the parlor, Mama,
they pay me by check and it doesn't bounce.
I'm giving a speech tonight. Do they
think I'm kidding? The walls I write
on are for sale now, but the message
is the same as I wrote in

blood on the jail house wall.
Energy flowing through me gets turned
into money and they take that back,
but the work remains, Mama, under
the carpet, in the walls, out
in the open. It goes on talking
after they've shut me up.

The poet dreams of a nice warm motel

Of course the plane is late,
two hours twisting bumpily
over Chicago in a droning grey funk
with the seatbelt sign on.
Either you are met by seven
young Marxists who want to know
at once What Is To Be Done
or one professor who says, What?
You have luggage? But I
parked in the no
parking zone.

Oh, we wouldn't want to put you
up at a motel, we here at
Southwestern Orthodontic Methodist,
we want you to feel homey:
drafty rooms where icicles
drip on your forehead, dorm cubicles
under the belltower where
the bells boom all night on each
quarter hour, rooms in faculty attics
two miles from a bathroom.

The bed

is a quarter inch mattress
flung upon springs of upended
razor blades: the mattress
is stuffed with fingernail
clippings and the feathers of buzzards.
If you roll over or cough it
sounds like a five-car collision.

The mattress is shaped that way
because our pet hippo Sweetie
likes to nap there. It's homey,
isn't it, meaning we're going to keep
you up with instant coffee
until two a.m. discussing why
we at Middle Fork State Teachers College
don't think you are truly great.

You'll love our dog Ogre,
she adores sleeping with guests
especially when she's in heat.
Don't worry, the children
will wake you. (They do.)
In the morning while all
fourteen children (the ones
with the flu and whooping cough
and, oh, you haven't had
the mumps – I mean, yet?) assault
you with tomahawks and strawberry
jam, you are asked, oh
would you like breakfast?
Naturally we never eat
breakfast ourselves, we believe
fasting purifies the system.
Have some cold tofu,
don't mind the mold.

No, we didn't order
your books, that's rampant
commercialism. We will call you
Miz Percy and make a joke about
women's libbers. The mike was run
over by a snowplow.
If we were too busy to put
up posters, we've obtained the
outdoor Greek Amphitheater
where you'll read to me and my wife.
If we blanketed five states
with announcements, we will be astounded
when five hundred cram into
the women's restroom we reserved.

Oh yes, the check will be four
months late. The next hungry poet
will be told, you'll be real comfortable
here, What's-her-name, that little Jew
from Detroit, she was through last year
and she found it real homey
in the Athens of the West.

Simple-song

When we are going toward someone we say
you are just like me
your thoughts are my brothers and sisters
word matches word
how easy to be together.

When we are leaving someone we say
how strange you are
we cannot communicate
we can never agree
how hard, hard and weary to be together.

We are not different nor alike
but each strangers in our leather bodies
sealed in skin and reaching out clumsy hands
and loving is an act
that cannot outlive
the open hand
the open eye
the door in the chest standing open.

Ancient wood

The wood speaks to me, said the carver,
I hear the song in it, of bear standing,
of wind shape that wants to cut through,
of snake undulating in the sand.

Wood is the stiff heart of the living
tree, the corpse left after its death.
We walk through our homes, our external
skeletons made of the bones of trees.

Some wood bends and some breaks.
Some we shape into baskets, wicker,
some into toothpicks, some into beams
that carry the weight of our lives.

But this petrified triangle beside
my computer is a different wonder:
an earthen hued rainbow of rock
shiny as ice, a knife once wood.

I could not carve it but it could
whittle me. I call it the poem
the wood made of its life, each
fat and lean year in shining rings.

The sugar and salts, the water
and sap are long transmuted
into a bright stone shape that has
outlasted not only tree but forest.

And whose creature am I?

At times characters from my novels swarm through me,
children of my mind, and possess me as dybbuks.
My own shabby memories they have plucked and eaten
till sometimes I cannot remember my own sorrows.
In all that I value there is a core of mystery,
in the seed that wriggles its new roots into the soil
and whose pale head bursts the surface,
in the dance where our bodies merge and reassemble,
in the starving baby whose huge glazing eyes
burned into my bones, in the look that passes
between predator and prey before the death blow.

I know of what rags and bones and clippings
from frothing newsprint and poisonous glue
my structures are built. Yet these creatures
I have improvised like golem walk off and thrive.
Between one and two thirds of our lives we spend
in darkness, and the little lights we turn on
burn little holes in that thick rich void.
We are never done with knowing or with gnawing,
but under the saying is whispering, touching
and silence. Out of a given set of atoms
we cast and recast the holy patterns new.

For Jeriann's hands

When I hug you, you are light as a grasshopper.
Your bones are ashwood the Indians used for bows.
You bend and spring back and can burn the touch,
a woman with hands that know how to pick things up.
Stiff as frozen rope words poke out
lopsided, in a fierce clothespin treble.
You move with a grace that is all function,
you move like a bow drawn taut and released.
Sometimes your wrists are transparent.
Sometimes an old buffalo man
frozen on the prairie stares from your face.
Your hair and eyes are the color of creek
running in the afternoon opaque under slanted sun.
You are stubborn and hardy as a rubber mat.
You are light as a paper airplane and as elegant
and you can fly.

The secret of moving heavy objects is balance, you said
in a grey loft full of your sculpture,
figures piercing or hung on boundaries,
leaping their thresholds, impaled on broken mirrors,
passing and gone into new space.
Objects born from you are mended, makeshift.
Their magic rides over rust and splinters and nails,
over shards of glass and cellophane beginning to rip.
Fragments of your work litter the banks of minor highways,
shattered faces of your icons lie on Hoboken junkyards,
float as smog over the East River,
grow black with the dust of abandoned coalbins.

One summer you made small rooms of wax
where people stood in taut ellipses staring and blind

with tenderness, with agony, with question and domestic terror.
They were candles burning.
You wanted to cast them in bronze but could not afford to.
The August sun melted them all.

The actors in your plays move in the dark
with masks and machines and chairs that trot and wail,
flimsy ragtag things that turn holy and whirl.
When you enter, we feel your presence burn blue,
no longer a woman, not wiry warm quick flesh
but a makeshift holy artifact
moving on the blank face of the dark as on a river:
ark, artifact, dancer of your own long breaking dance
which makes itself through you
fiercely, totally passing in light
leaving you thin and darkened as burnt glass.

The answer to all problems

We aren't available, we can't talk to you
right now, but you can talk to us, we say,
but think of the astonishment if machines
suddenly spoke truth: What do you want?

You'd best have a damned good reason for bothering
me, intruding on my silence. If you're bored,
read a good book. Masturbate on your own time.
Call weather or your mother or a talk show.

If you're a creditor, I've just been cremated.
If you're my ex, I'm fucking a perfect body

in Acapulco. Hi, I'm too shy to answer.
I'm scared of obscene calls. I'm paranoid.

I'm sharing a bottle of wine and a loaf of bread
with my lover, our flesh smokes with desire,
our lips brush, our clothes uncoil hissing,
and you have a problem? Try prayer.

Hi obtuse one, it may be eleven on the West Coast
but it's two a.m. here and as you listen
a pitch too high for you to hear is giving
you herpes and melting your elastic and velcro.

Hi, this is the machine. My person is standing
two feet away to hear if you're worth the effort.
Hi. If you hang up without leaving a message
your teeth will loosen overnight. I hate drones.

Hi, can my machine call your machine
and make an appointment? Can my machine
mate with yours and breed Walkmans?
Hi, my humans have been murdered and cannot come.

Athena in the front lines

Only accidents preserve.
Athene Promachos, warrior goddess thirty feet tall,
no longer exists. Phidias
made her between wars in ruins
of a fort that had not kept the enemy out.
Making is an attack too, on bronze, on air, on time.
Sailors out on the Argo-Saronic
of gull and dolphin and bone-dry island
could see the sunlight creaking on her helmet.

A thousand years she stood over fire and mud,
then hauled as booty to Constantinople,
where the Crusaders, bouncy legionnaires
on the town, melted her down for coins.

These words are pebbles
sucked from mouth to mouth since Chaucer.
I don't believe the Etruscans or the Mayans
lacked poets, only victories.
Manuscripts under glass, women's quilts packed away
lie in the attics of museums sealed from the streets
where the tactical police are clubbing the welfare mothers.
There are no cameras, so it is not real.

Wring the stones of the hillside
for the lost plays of Sophocles they heard.
Art is nonaccident. Like love, it is
a willed tension up through the mind
balancing thrust and inertia, energy
stored in a bulb. Then the golden
trumpet of the narcissus pokes up
willfully into the sun, focusing the world.

The epigraphs stabbed the Song of Songs
through the smoking heart (The Church
Prepares for Her Bridegroom). The seven hundred
thousand fifty second tourist stared
the Venus de Milo into a brassiere ad.
Generations of women wrote poems and hid
them in drawers, because an able
woman is a bad woman. They expired
leaking radioactivity among pastel underwear.

A woman scribbling for no one doodles,
dabbles in madness, dribbles shame.
Art requires a plaza in the mind, a space
lit by the sun of regard. That tension

between maker and audience, that feedback,
that force field of interest, sustains
an I less guilty that Ego, who can utter
the truths of vision and nightmare,
the truths that spill like raw egg from the
cracking of body on body, the thousand
soft and slimy names of death, the songs
of the blind fish that swim
the caverns of bone, the songs
of the hawks who soar and stoop grappling
and screaming through the crystalline
skies of the forehead.

Though the cod stifle in the seas, though
the rivers thicken to shit, still
writing implies faith in someone listening,
different in content but not in need
from the child who cries in the night.

Making is an attack on dying, on chaos,
on blind inertia, on the second law
of thermodynamics, on indifference, on cold,
on contempt, on the silence
that does not follow the chord resolved,
the sentence spoken, but the something
that cannot be said. Perhaps there are no
words yet; perhaps the words bend the thought
back on itself; perhaps the words can be said
but cannot yet be heard, and so
the saying arches through air and crumbles.

Making is an act, but survival
is luck, caught in history
like a moth trapped in the subway.
There is nothing to do but make well,
finish and let go. Words

live, words die
in the mouths of everybody.

For the young who want to

Talent is what they say
you have after the novel
is published and favorably
reviewed. Beforehand what
you have is a tedious
delusion, a hobby like knitting.

Work is what you have done
after the play is produced
and the audience claps.
Before that friends keep asking
when you are planning to go
out and get a job.

Genius is what they know you
had after the third volume
of remarkable poems. Earlier
they accuse you of withdrawing,
ask why you don't have a baby,
call you a bum.

The reason people want M.F.A.'s,
take workshops with fancy names
when all you can really
learn is a few techniques,
typing instructions and somebody else's mannerisms

is that every artist lacks
a license to hang on the wall
like your optician, your vet
proving you may be a clumsy sadist
whose fillings fall into the stew
but you're certified a dentist.

The real writer is one
who really writes. Talent
is an invention like phlogiston
after the fact of fire.
Work is its own cure. You have to
like it better than being loved.

A GARDEN IS ALL WE WILL EVER KNOW
OF PARADISE

Seedlings in the mail

Like mail order brides
they are lacking in glamor.
Drooping and frail and wispy,
they are orphaned waifs of some green catastrophe
from which only they have been blown to safety
swaddled in a few wraiths of sphagnum moss.

Windbreaks, orchards, forests of the mind
they huddle in the dirt
smaller than our cats.
The catalog said they would grow
to stand one hundred feet tall.
I could plant them in the bathroom.
I could grow them in window pots,
twelve trees to an egg carton.
I could dig four into the pockets of my jeans.
I could wear some in my hair
or my armpits.
Ah, for people like us, followed
by forwarding addresses and dossiers and limping causes
it takes a crazy despairing faith
full of teeth as a jack o'lantern
to plant pine and fir and beech
for somebody else's grandchildren
if there are any.

The daily life of the worker bee

We breed plants, order seeds from
the opulent pornography of the catalogs,
weed, fertilize, water,
but the flowers do not shine for us.

Forty days of life, working like a housewife
with six kids in diapers, at it like an oil rig pumping.
With condescension we pass on: busy as a bee.

Yet for them the green will of the plants
has thrust out colors, odors, the shapely trumpets and cups.
As the sun strikes the petals, the flower uncurls,
the bees come glinting and singing.

Now she crawls into the crimson rooms of the rose
where perfume reddens the air to port wine.
Marigolds sturdy in the grass barking like golden chow dogs
cry their wares to her. Enter. Devour me!
In her faceted eyes each image reverberates.
Cumulus clouds of white phlox
pile up for her in the heat of the sunburnt day.
Down into the soft well of the summer lilies,
cerise, citron, umber, rufous orange,
anthers with their palate of pollen
tremble as she enters.
She rubs her quivering fur
into each blue bell of the borage.
In the chamber of the peony she is massaged with silk.

Forty days she is drunk with nectar.
Each blossom utters fragrance to entice her,
offers up its soft flanks, its maddening colors,
its sweet and pungent fluids.

She never mates; her life is orgasm of all senses.
She dies one morning exhausted in the lap of the rose.
Like love letters turned up in an attic trunk
her honey remains to sweeten us.

Digging in

This fall you will taste carrots
you planted, you thinned, you mulched,
you weeded and watered. You don't
know yet they will taste like yours,
not others', not mine.
This earth is yours as you love it.

We drink the water of this hill
and give our garbage to its soil.
We haul thatch for it and seaweed.
Out of it rise supper,
roses for the bedroom,
herbs for your next cold.

Your flesh grows from this hill
like the maple trees. Its sweetness
is baked by this sun. Your eyes
have taken in sea and the light leaves
of the locust and the dark bristles
of the pine.

When we work in the garden you say
that now it feels sexual, the plants
pushing through us, the shivering
of the leaves. As we make love

the oaks bend over us,
the hill listens.

The cats come and sit on the foot
of the bed to watch us.
Afterwards they purr.
The tomatoes grow faster and the beans.
You are learning to live in circles
as well as straight lines.

Attack of the squash people

And thus the people every year
in the valley of humid July
did sacrifice themselves
to the long green phallic god
and eat and eat and eat.

They're coming, they're on us,
the long striped gourds, the silky
babies, the hairy adolescents,
the lumpy vast adults
like the trunks of green elephants.
Recite fifty zucchini recipes!

Zucchini tempura; creamed soup;
sauté with olive oil and cumin,
tomatoes, onion; frittata;
casserole of lamb; baked
topped with cheese; marinated;
stuffed; stewed; driven
through the heart like a stake.

Get rid of old friends; they too
have gardens and full trunks.
Look for newcomers: befriend
them in the post office, unload
on them and run. Stop tourists
in the street. Take truckloads
to the city. Give to your Red Cross.
Beg on the highway: please
take my zucchini, I have a crippled
mother at home with heartburn.

Sneak out before dawn to drop
them in other people's gardens,
in baby buggies at churchdoors.
Shot, smuggling zucchini into
mailboxes, a federal offense.

With a suave reptilian glitter
you bask among your raspy
fronds sudden and huge as
alligators. You give and give
too much, like summer days
limp with heat, thunderstorms
bursting their bags on our heads,
as we salt and freeze and pickle
for the too little to come.

Baboons in the perennial bed

Even after common sense whittles ambition
I always order too many seeds, bulbs, corms.
What's the lure? Why am I torn between
cutting the lily for my bedside and savoring
it daily on its pedestal of crisp leaves?

They rouse and sate the senses, touch,
sight, scent, the wild shagginess and precise
sculpted lines, the shadings of color from clang
to sigh. Yet I think what moves underneath
is pleased envy at their flagrancy.

They wave their sexual organs in the air,
the plants, colored far more freely than the hind-
quarters of baboons. We who are raised to shame
for the moist orchid between our thighs
must wish we were as certain of our beauty.

Apple sauce for Eve

Those old daddies cursed you and us in you,
damned for your curiosity: for your sin
was wanting knowledge. To try, to taste,
to take into the body, into the brain
and turn each thing, each sign, each factoid
round and round as new facets glint and white
fractures into colors and the image breaks
into crystal fragments that pierce the nerves
while the brain casts the chips into patterns.

Each experiment sticks a finger deep in the pie,
dares existence, blows a horn in the ear
of belief, lets the nasty and difficult brats
of real questions into the still air
of the desiccated parlor of stasis.
What we all know to be true, constant,
melts like frost landscapes on a window
in a jet of steam. How many last words
in how many dead languages would translate into,
But what happens if I, and Whoops!

We see Adam wagging his tail, good dog, good
dog, while you and the snake shimmy up the tree,
lab partners in a dance of will and hunger,
that thirst not of the flesh but of the brain.
Men always think women are wanting sex,
cock, snake, when it is the world she's after.
Then birth trauma for the first conceived kid
of the ego, I think therefore I am, I
kick the tree, who am I, why am I,
going, going to die, die, die.

You are indeed the mother of invention,
the first scientist. Your name means
life: finite, dynamic, swimming against
the current of time, tasting, testing,
eating knowledge like any other nutrient.
We are all the children of your bright hunger.
We are all products of that first experiment,
for if death was the worm in that apple,
the seeds were freedom and the flowering of choice.

Available light

Ripe and runny as perfect Brie, at this age
appetites mature rampant and allowed.
I am wet as a salt marsh under the flood tide
of the full solstice moon and dry as salt itself
that draws the superfluous juice from the tissues
to leave the desiccated butterfly wing intact.

I know myself as I know the four miles I walk
every morning, the sky like ice formed on skim
milk, the sky dappled and fat and rolling, never
the same two hours later. I know there are rooms
upon caverns opening off corridors I will never
enter, as well as those I'll be thrust into.

I am six with my mother watching Clippers
take off for Lisbon. I am nine and the President
whose voice is a personal god is dying in the radio.
I am twelve and coming while I mutter yes, yes,
of course, this is what the bones grow around to hold.
I am twenty-four as my best friend bleeds her life out.

At any moment I find myself under the water of my
past trying to breathe in that thick refracted medium.
At any moment a new voice is speaking me like a p.a.
system that one day amplifies a lecture on newts
and the next day jazz. I am always finding new
beings in me like otters swimming in the soup.

I have friends who gave themselves to Marx, to Freud,
to A.A., to Christianity or Buddhism or Goddess
religions, to the Party or the Lord or the Lover.
As a Jew, I have a god who returns me to myself
uncleaned, to be used again, since forgiveness must
be sung but changes not one needle falling from the pine.

As consequences show their lengthened teeth
from the receding gums, we hunger for the larger
picture, the longer view, and yet and yet
I cannot augment the natural curve of earth
except by including the moth and the mammoth,
the dark river percolating through the sea

built rock, the dense memories of shell
and sediment, the million deaths recorded
in each inch; the warm funky breath
of Leviathan as he breached off the portside;
people in boots struggling to shove the pilot
whales free that a storm surge grounded.

In winter the light is red and short.
The sun hangs its wizened rosehip in the oaks.
By midafternoon night is folding in.
The ground is locked against us like a door.
Yet faces shine so the eyes stretch for them
and tracks in the snow are etched, calligraphy

I learn by rote and observation, patient
the way I am finally learning Hebrew
at fifty, forgiving my dead parents
who saw squinting by their own scanty light.
By four o'clock I must give up the woods,
come in, turn on every lamp to read.

Later when the moon has set I go out
and let the spears of Sirius and Rigel
pierce the ivory of my skull and enter
my blood like glowing isotopes of distance.
As I stand in the cold vault of the night
I see more and fainter stars as my eyes

clear or my blood cools. The barred owl
hoots. The skunk prances past me to stir

the compost pile with her sharp nails.
A lithe weasel flicks across the cul de sac.
Even the dead of winter: it seethes with more
than I can ever live to name and speak.

Toad dreams

(*That afternoon the dream of the toads rang through the elms by Little
River and affected the thoughts of men, though they were not conscious
that they heard it. — Henry Thoreau*)

The dream of toads: we rarely
credit what we consider lesser
life with emotions big as ours,
but we are easily distracted,
abstracted. People sit nibbling
before television's flicker watching
ghosts chase balls and each other
while the skunk is out risking grisly
death to cross the highway to mate;
while the fox scales the wire fence
where it knows the shotgun lurks
to taste the sweet blood of a hen.
Birds are greedy little bombs
bursting to give voice to appetite.
I had a cat who died of love.
Dogs trail their masters across continents. We are far too busy
to be starkly simple in passion.
We will never dream the intense
wet spring lust of the toads.

The common living dirt

The small ears prick on the bushes,
furry buds, shoots tender and pale.
The swamp maples blow scarlet.
Color teases the corner of the eye,
delicate gold, chartreuse, crimson,
mauve speckled, just dashed on.

The soil stretches naked. All winter
hidden under the down comforter of snow,
delicious now, rich in the hand
as chocolate cake, the fragrant busy
soil the worm passes through her gut
and the beetle swims in like a lake.

As I kneel to tuck the seeds in
careful as stitching, I am in love.
You are the bed we all sleep on.
You are the food we eat, the food
we ate, the food we will become.
We are walking trees rooted in you.

You can live thousands of years
undressing in the spring your black
body, your red body, your brown body
penetrated by the rain. Here
is the goddess unveiled,
the earth opening her strong thighs.

Yet you grow exhausted with bearing
too much, too soon, too often, just
as a woman wears through like an old rug.
We have contempt for what we spring
from. Dirt, we say, you're dirt
as if we were not all your children.

[193]

We have lost the simplest gratitude.
We lack the knowledge we showed ten
thousand years past, that you live
a goddess but mortal, that what we take
must be returned, that the poison we drop
in you will stunt our children's growth.

Tending a plot of your flesh binds
me as nothing ever could, to the seasons,
to the will of the plants, clamorous
in their green tenderness. What
calls louder than the cry of a field
of corn ready, or trees of ripe peaches?

I worship on my knees, laying
seeds in you, that worship rooted
in need, in hunger, in kinship,
flesh of the planet with my own flesh,
a ritual of compost, a litany of manure.
My garden's a chapel, but a meadow

gone wild in grass and flower
is a cathedral. How you seethe
with little quick ones, vole, field
mouse, shrew and mole in their thousands,
rabbit and woodchuck. In you rest
the jewels of the genes wrapped in seed.

Power warps because it means joy
in standing over; because it means
forgetting how we too starve, break
like a corn stalk in the wind, how we
die like the spinach of drought,
how what poisons the vole slays us.

Because you can die of overwork, because
you can die of the fire that melts

rock, because you can die of the poison
that kills the beetle and the slug,
we must come again to worship you
on our knees, the common living dirt.

Six underrated pleasures

1. FOLDING SHEETS

They must be clean.
There ought to be two of you
to talk as you work, your
eyes and hands meeting.
They can be crisp, a little rough
and fragrant from the line;
or hot from the dryer
as from an oven. A silver
grey kitten with amber
eyes to dart among
the sheets and wrestle and leap out
helps. But mostly pleasure
lies in the clean linen
slapping into shape.
Whenever I fold a fitted sheet
making the moves that are like
closing doors, I feel my mother.
The smell of clean laundry is hers.

2. PICKING POLE BEANS

Gathering tomatoes has no art
to it. Their ripe redness shouts.
But the scarlet runner beans twine

high and jungly on their tripods.
You must reach in delicately,
pinch off the sizable beans
but leave the babies to swell
into flavor. It is hide-and-seek,
standing knee deep in squash
plants running, while the bees
must be carefully disentangled
from your hair. Early you may see
the hummingbird, but best to wait
until the dew burns off.
Basket on your arm, your fingers
go swimming through the raspy leaves
to find prey just their size.
Then comes the minor zest
of nipping the ends off with your nails
and snapping them in pieces,
their retorts like soft pistolry.
Then eat the littlest raw.

3. TAKING A HOT BATH

Surely nobody has ever decided
to go on a diet while in a tub.
The body is beautiful stretched
out under water wavering.

It suggests a long island of pleasure,
whole seascapes of calm sensual
response, the nerves as gentle fronds
of waterweed swaying in warm currents.

Then if ever we must love ourselves
in the amniotic fluid floating
a ship at anchor in a perfect
protected blood-warm tropical bay.

The water enters us and the minor
pains depart, supplanted guests,
the aches, the strains, the chills.
Muscles open like hungry clams.

Born again from my bath like a hot
sweet-tempered, sweet-smelling baby,
I am ready to seize sleep like a milky breast
or start climbing my day hand over hand.

4. SLEEPING WITH CATS

I am at once source
and sink of heat: giver
and taker. I am a vast
soft mountain of slow breathing.
The smells I exude soothe them:
the lingering odor of sex,
of soap, even of perfume,
its afteraroma sunk into skin
mingling with sweat and the traces
of food and drink.

They are curled into flowers
of fur, they are coiled
hot seashells of flesh
in my armpit, around my head
a dark sighing halo.
They are plastered to my side,
a poultice fixing sore muscles
better than a heating pad.
They snuggle up to my sex
purring. They embrace my feet.

Some cats I place like a pillow.
In the morning they rest where

I arranged them, still sleeping.
Some cats start at my head
and end between my legs
like a textbook lover. Some
slip out to prowl the living room
patrolling, restive, then
leap back to fight about
hegemony over my knees.

Every one of them cares
passionately where they sleep
and with whom.
Sleeping together is a euphemism
for people but tantamount
to marriage for cats.
Mammals together we snuggle
and snore through the cold nights
while the stars swing round
the pole and the great horned
owl hunts for flesh like ours.

5. PLANTING BULBS

No task could be easier.
Just dig the narrow hole,
drop in a handful of bone
meal and place the bulb
like a swollen brown garlic
clove full of hidden resources.

Their skin is the paper
of brown bags. The smooth
pale flesh peeks through.
Three times its height
is its depth, a parable
against hard straining.

The art is imagining
the spring landscape poking
through chrysanthemum, falling
leaves, withered brown lushness
of summer. The lines drawn
now, the colors mixed

will pop out of the soil
after the snow sinks from sight
into it. The circles,
the casual grace of tossed handfuls,
the soldierly rows will stand,
the colors sing sweet or sour.

When the first sharp ears
poke out, you are again
more audience than actor,
as if someone said, Close
your eyes and draw a picture.
Now open them and look.

6. CANNING

We pour a mild drink each,
turn on the record player,
Beethoven perhaps or Vivaldi,
opera, and then together
in the steamy kitchen we put up
tomatoes, peaches, grapes, pears.

Each fruit has a different
ritual: popping the grapes
out of the skins like little
eyeballs, slipping the fuzz
from the peaches and seeing
the blush painted on the flesh beneath.

It is part game: What shall
we magic wand this into?
Peach conserve, chutney, jam,
brandied peaches. Tomatoes
turn juice, sauce hot or mild
or spicy, canned, ketchup.

Vinegars, brandies, treats
for the winter: pleasure
deferred. Canning is thrift
itself in sensual form,
surplus made beautiful, light
and heat caught in a jar.

I find my mother sometimes
issuing from the steam, aproned,
red faced, her hair up in a net.
Since her death we meet usually
in garden or kitchen. Ghosts
come reliably to savors, I learn.

In the garden your ashes,
in the kitchen your knowledge.
Little enough we can save
from the furnace of the sun
while the bones grow brittle as paper
and the hair itself turns ashen.

But what we can put by, we do
with gaiety and invention
while the music laps round us
like dancing light, but Mother,
this pleasure is only deferred.
We eat it all before it spoils.

The seven of pentacles
(from 'Laying Down the Tower', a sequence based on a Tarot reading)

Under a sky the color of pea soup
she is looking at her work growing away there
actively, thickly like grapevines or pole beans
as things grow in the real world, slowly enough.
If you tend them properly, if you mulch, if you water,
if you provide birds that eat insects a home and winter food,
if the sun shines and you pick off caterpillars,
if the praying mantis comes and the lady bugs and the bees,
then the plants flourish, but at their own internal clock.

Connections are made slowly, sometimes they grow
    underground.
You cannot tell always by looking what is happening.
More than half a tree is spread out in the soil under your feet.
Penetrate quietly as the earthworm that blows no trumpet.
Fight persistently as the creeper that brings down the oak.
Spread like the squash plant that overruns the garden.
Gnaw in the dark and use the sun to make sugar.

Weave real connections, create real nodes, build real homes.
Live a life you can endure; make love that is loving.
Keep tangling and interweaving and taking more in,
a thicket and bramble wilderness to the outside but to us
interconnected with rabbit runs and burrows and lairs.

Live as if you liked yourself and it may happen:
reach out, keep reaching out, keep bringing in.
This is how we are going to live for a long time: not always,
for every gardener knows that after the digging, after the
    planting,
after the long season of tending and growth, the harvest comes.

The sun

(The 'outcome' poem of the Tarot sequence, 'Laying Down the Tower')

Androgynous child whose hair curls into flowers,
naked you ride a horse without saddle or bridle
easy between your thighs from the walled garden outward.
Coarse sunflowers of desire whose seeds birds crack open
nod upon your journey, child of the morning whose sun
can only be born from us who strain bleeding to give birth.
Grow into your horse, let there be
no more riders or ridden.

Child, where are you heading with arms spread wide
as a shore, have I been there, have I seen that land shining
like sun spangles on clean water rippling?
I do not know your dances, I cannot translate your tongue
to words I use, your pleasures are strange to me
as the rites of bees: yet you are the yellow flower
of a melon vine growing out of my belly
though it climbs up where I cannot see in the strong light.

My eyes cannot decipher those shapes of children or burning
    clouds
who are not what we are: they go barefoot like savages;
they have computers as household pets; they are seven sexes
and only one sex; they do not own or lease or control.
They are of one body and of tribes. They are private as shamans
learning each her own magic at the teats of stones and trees.
They are all technicians and peasants.
They do not forget their birthright of self
or their mane of animal pride
dancing in and out through the gates of the body standing wide.

A bear lumbering, I waddle into the fields of their work games.
We are stunted slaves mumbling over the tales
of dragons our masters tell us, but we will be free.
Our children will be free of us, uncomprehending
as we of those shufflers in caves who scraped for fire
and banded together at last to hunt the saber-toothed tiger,
the giant cave bear, predators
that had penned them up cowering too long.

The sun is rising, feel it: the air smells fresh.
I cannot look in the sun's face, its brightness blinds me,
but from my own shadow becoming distinct
I know that now at last
it is beginning to grow light.

THE LUNAR CYCLE

The lunar calendar with which I am most familiar is the Jewish calendar, but I used the Celtic names, out of homage to Nancy Passmore and her annual publication of The Lunar Calendar, and because more women (and more poets generally, thanks to Robert Graves) know about the lunar months by their Celtic names and associated trees.

The moon is always female

The moon is always female and so
am I although often in this vale
of razorblades I have wished I could
put on and take off my sex like a dress
and why not? Do men wear their sex
always? The priest, the doctor, the teacher
all tell us they come to their professions
neuter as clams and the truth is
when I work I am pure as an angel
tiger and clear is my eye and hot
my brain and silent all the whining
grunting piglets of the appetites.
For we were priests to the goddesses
to whom were fashioned the first altars
of clumsy stone on stone and leaping animal
in the wombdark caves, long before men
put on skirts and masks to scare babies.
For we were healers with herbs and poultices
with our milk and careful fingers
long before they began learning to cut up
the living by making jokes at corpses.
For we were making sounds from our throats
and lips to warn and encourage the helpless
young long before schools were built
to teach boys to obey and be bored and kill.

I wake in a strange slack empty bed
of a motel, shaking like dry leaves
the wind rips loose, and in my head
is bound a girl of twelve whose female
organs all but the numb womb are being
cut from her with a knife. Clitoridectomy,

whatever Latin name you call it, in a quarter
of the world girl children are so maimed
and I think of her and I cannot stop.
And I think of her and I cannot stop.

If you are a woman you feel the knife in the words.
If you are a man, then at age four or else
at twelve you are seized and held down
and your penis is cut off. You are left
your testicles but they are sewed to your
crotch. When your spouse buys you, you
are torn or cut open so that your precious
semen can be siphoned out, but of course
you feel nothing. But pain. But pain.

For the uses of men we have been butchered
and crippled and shut up and carved open
under the moon that swells and shines
and shrinks again into nothingness, pregnant
and then waning toward its little monthly
death. The moon is always female but the sun
is female only in lands where females
are let into the sun to run and climb.

A woman is screaming and I hear her.
A woman is bleeding and I see her
bleeding from the mouth, the womb, the breasts
in a fountain of dark blood of dismal
daily tedious sorrow quite palatable
to the taste of the mighty and taken for granted
that the bread of domesticity be baked
of our flesh, that the hearth be built
of our bones of animals kept for meat and milk,
that we open and lie under and weep.
I want to say over the names of my mothers
like the stones of a path I am climbing
rock by slippery rock into the mists.

Never even at knife point have I wanted
or been willing to be or become a man.
I want only to be myself and free.

I am waiting for the moon to rise. Here
I squat, the whole country with its steel
mills and its coal mines and its prisons
at my back and the continent tilting
up into mountains and torn by shining lakes
all behind me on this scythe of straw,
a sand bar cast on the ocean waves, and I
wait for the moon to rise red and heavy
in my eyes. Chilled, cranky, fearful
in the dark I wait and I am all the time
climbing slippery rocks in a mist while
far below the waves crash in the sea caves;
I am descending a stairway under the groaning
sea while the black waters buffet me
like rockweed to and fro.

I have swum the upper waters leaping
in dolphin's skin for joy equally into the
necessary air and the tumult of the powerful wave.
I am entering the chambers I have visited.
I have floated through them sleeping and sleep-
walking and waking, drowning in passion
festooned with green bladderwrack of misery.
I have wandered these chambers in the rock
where the moon freezes the air and all hair
is black or silver. Now I will tell you
what I have learned lying under the moon
naked as women do: now I will tell you
the changes of the high and lower moon.
Out of necessity's hard stones we suck
what water we can and so we have survived,
women born of women. There is knowing

with the teeth as well as knowing with
the tongue and knowing with the fingertips
as well as knowing with words and with all
the fine flickering of the brain.

Right to life
(SAILLE)

A woman is not a pear tree
thrusting her fruit in mindless fecundity
into the world. Even pear trees bear
heavily one year and rest and grow the next.
An orchard gone wild drops few warm rotting
fruit in the grass but the trees stretch
high and wiry gifting the birds forty
feet up among inch long thorns
broken atavistically from the smooth wood.

A woman is not a basket you place
your buns in to keep them warm. Not a brood
hen you can slip duck eggs under.
Not a purse holding the coins of your
descendants till you spend them in wars.
Not a bank where your genes gather interest
and interesting mutations in the tainted rain.

You plant corn and you harvest
it to eat or sell. You put the lamb
in the pasture to fatten and haul it in
to butcher for chops. You slice
the mountain in two for a road and gouge
the high plains for coal and the waters
run muddy for miles and years.
Fish die but you do not call them yours
unless you planned to eat them.

Now you legislate mineral rights in a woman.
You lay claim to her pasture for grazing,
fields for growing babies like iceberg
lettuce. You value children so dearly
that none ever go hungry, none weep
with no one to tend them when mothers
work, none lack fresh fruit,
none chew lead or cough to death and your
foster homes are empty. Every noon the best
restaurants serve poor children steaks.

At this moment at nine o'clock a *partera*
is performing a table top abortion on an
unwed mother in Texas who can't get Medicaid
any longer. In five days she will die
of tetanus and her little daughter will cry
and be taken away. Next door a husband
and wife are sticking pins in the son
they did not want. They will explain
for hours how wicked he is,
how he wants discipline.

We are all born of woman. In the rose
of the womb we suckled our mother's blood
and every baby born has a right to love
like a seedling to sun. Every baby born
unloved, unwanted is a bill that will come
due in twenty years with interest, an anger
that must find a target, a pain that will
beget pain. A decade downstream a child
screams, a woman falls, a synagogue is torched,
a firing squad is summoned, a button
is pushed and the world burns.

I will choose what enters me, what becomes
flesh of my flesh. Without choice, no politics,

no ethics lives. I am not your cornfield,
not your uranium mine, not your calf
for fattening, not your cow for milking.
You may not use me as your factory.
Priests and legislators do not hold
shares in my womb or my mind.
This is my body. If I give it to you
I want it back. My life
is a non-negotiable demand.

May apple
(UATH)

Hawthorn: spines long as my little finger
that glint in the sun before the leaves come out,
small white flowers like the wild rose
and fruits people don't eat. Virginity.

Not the hymen it took a week to drill through.
All at sixteen I could concentrate on
was what happened how and would it soon
while my mind turned into chewed bubblegum
and my periods racked me like earthquakes.

No, virginity in the old sense of a woman
unmated and not mating: solitude. A state
I have passed in and out of, the nature
of the dreaming mind nobody courts.

State of my cats when they are neither
in heat nor pregnant but predators, players,
brooding elegant gods. Sitting paws folded

and facing they blink courteously
and contemplate mathematical laws.

Eyes alter us by their observant gaze.
We are never the same after someone
has first loved us. The self the other
sees hangs in the mirror at least part time.

The innocence lost is living for myself,
ignorant as a wild hawthorn how to allure,
flatter, please and in what light arrange
the hair and limbs like a bouquet of white
flowers, dark twigs snipped off the tree.

Alone I am clear as clean ice.
I sleep short hours, stop cooking sauces,
and every day like a desert monk I contemplate
death in each apple core and woodash.

Alone I am twelve years old and eighty.
Alone I am sexless as a pine board.
Alone I am invisible to myself as carbon
dioxide. I touch myself often and then less
as my dreams darken to stained glass allegories.

Alone I find old fears preserved like hiking
boots at the bottom of the closet in a box,
my feet having shaped them just perfect to fit
and eight years later I set off in them to climb.

I become nocturnal. My eyes glow in the dark.
The moist rich parts of me contract underground
into tubers. What stands up still is strong
but crotchety, the village witch people come to
with savory troubles, all ears and teeth.

Shadows of the burning
(DUIR)

Oak burns steady and hot and long
and fires of oak are traditional tonight
but we light a fire of pitch pine
which burns well enough in the salt wind
whistling while ragged flames lick the dark
casting our shadows high as the dunes.

Come into the fire and catch,
come in, come in. Fire that burns
and leaves entire, the silver flame
of the moon, trembling mercury laying
on the waves a highway to the abyss,
the full roaring furnace of the sun at zenith
of the year and potency, midsummer's eve.

Come dance in the fire, come in.
This is the briefest night and just
under the ocean the fires of the sun
roll toward us. Already your skin is dark,
already your wiry curls are tipped with gold
and my black hair begins to redden.

How often I have leapt into that fire,
how often burned like a torch, my hair
streaming sparks, and wakened to weep
ashes. I have said, love is a downer we take,
love is a habit like sucking on death tit cigarettes,
love is a bastard art. Instead of painting
or composing, we compose a beloved.
When you love for a living, I have said,
you're doomed to early retirement without benefits.

For women have died and worms have eaten them
and just for love. Love of the wrong man or
the right. Death from abortion, from the first
child or the eighteenth, death at the stake
for loving a woman or freedom or the wrong
deity. Death at the open end of a gun
from a jealous man, a vengeful man,
Othello's fingers. Henry's ax.

It is romance I loathe, the swooning moon
of June which croons to the tune of every goon.
Venus on the half shell without the reek
of seaweed preferred to Artemis of the rows
of breasts like a sow and the bow
ready in her hand that kills and the herbs
that save in childbirth.

Ah, my name hung once like a can
on an ink stained girl blue as skim milk
lumpy with elbows, spiky with scruples,
who knelt in a tower raised of Shelley's bones
praying my demon lover asceticism
to grant one icy vision.

I found my body in the arms of lovers
and woke in the flesh alive, astounded
like a corpse sitting up in a judgment
day painting. My own five hound senses
turned on me, chased me, tore me
head from trunk. Thumb and liver
and jaw on the bloody hillside
twanged like frogs on the night I am alive!

A succession of lovers like a committee
of Congress in slow motion put me back
together, a thumb under my ear, the ear

in an armpit, the head sprouting feet.
Kaleidoscope where glass sparks pierced
my eyes, in love's funhouse I was hung
a mirror of flesh reflecting flaccid ideas
of men scouting their mothers through my womb,
a labyrinth of years in other
people's thoroughly furnished rooms.

I built myself like a house a poor family
puts up in the country: first the foundation
under a tarred flat roof like a dugout,
then the well in the spring and you get
electricity connected and maybe the next
fall you seal in two rooms and add some
plumbing but all the time you're living
there constructing your way out of a slum.
Yet for whom is this built if not to be shared
with the quick steps and low voice of love?

I cherish friendship and loving that starts
in liking but the body is the church
where I praise and bless and am blessed.
My strength and my weakness are twins
in the same womb, mirrored dancers under
water, the dark and light side of the moon.
I know how truly my seasons have turned
cold and hot
around that lion-bodied sun.

Come step into the fire, come in,
come in, dance in the flames of the festival
of the strongest sun at the mountain top
of the year when the wheel starts down.
Dance through me as I through you.
Here in the heart of fire in the caves
of the ancient body we are aligned

[216]

with the stars wheeling, the midges swarming
in the humid air like a nebula, with the clams
who drink the tide and the heartwood clock
of the oak and the astronomical clock
in the blood thundering through the great heart
of the albatross. Our cells are burning
each a little furnace powered by the sun
and the moon pulls the sea of our blood.
This night the sun and moon dance
and you and I dance in the fire of which
we are the logs, the matches and the flames.

The sabbath of mutual respect
(TINNE)

In the natural year come two thanksgivings,
the harvest of summer and the harvest of fall,
two times when we eat and drink and remember our dead
under the golden basin of the moon of plenty.

Abundance, Habondia, food for the winter,
too much now and survival later. After
the plant bears, it dies into seed.
The blowing grasses nourish us, wheat
and corn and rye, millet and rice, oat
and barley and buckwheat, all the serviceable
grasses of the pasture that the cow grazes,
the lamb, the horse, the goat; the grasses
that quicken into meat and cheese and milk,
the humble necessary mute vegetable bees,
the armies of the grasses waving their

golden banners of ripe seed.
                              The sensual
round fruit gleams with the sun
stored in its sweetness.
                         The succulent
ephemera of the summer garden, bloodwarm
tomatoes, tender small squash, crisp
beans, the milky corn, the red peppers
exploding like cherry bombs in the mouth.

We praise abundance by eating of it,
reveling in choice on a table set with roses
and lilies and phlox, zucchini and lettuce
and eggplant before the long winter
of root crops.
               Fertility and choice:
every row dug in spring means weeks
of labor. Plant too much and the seedlings
choke in weeds as the warm rain soaks them.
The goddess of abundance Habondia is also
the spirit of labor and choice.
                                In another
life, dear sister, I too would bear six fat
children. In another life, my sister, I too
would love another woman and raise one child
together as if that pushed from both our wombs.
In another life, sister, I too would dwell
solitary and splendid as a lighthouse on the rocks
or be born to mate for life like the faithful goose.
Praise all our choices. Praise any woman
who chooses, and make safe her choice.

Habondia, Artemis, Cybele, Demeter, Ishtar,
Aphrodite, Au Set, Hecate, Themis, Lilith,
Thea, Gaia, Bridgit, the Great Grandmother of Us
All, Yemanja, Cerridwen, Freya, Corn Maiden,

[218]

Mawu, Amaterasu, Maires, Nut, Spider-Woman,
Neith, Au Zit, Hathor, Inanna, Shin Moo,
Diti, Arinna, Anath, Tiamat, Astoreth:
the names flesh out our histories, our choices,
our passions and what we will never embody
but pass by with respect. When I consecrate
my body in the temple of our history,
when I pledge myself to remain empty
and clear for the voices coming through
I do not choose for you or lessen your choice.

Habondia, the real abundance, is the power
to say yes and to say no, to open
and to close, to take or to leave
and not to be taken by force or law
or fear or poverty or hunger.
To bear children or not to bear by choice
is holy. To bear children unwanted
is to be used like a public sewer.
To be sterilized unchosen is to have
your heart cut out. To love women
is holy and holy is the free love of men
and precious to live taking whichever comes
and precious to live unmated as a peachtree.

Praise the lives you did not choose.
They will heal you, tell your story, fight
for you. You eat the bread of their labor.
You drink the wine of their joy. I tell you
after I went under the surgeon's knife
for the laparoscopy, I felt like a trumpet
an Amazon was blowing sonorous charges on.
Then my womb learned to open on the full
moon without pain and my pleasure deepened
till my body shuddered like troubled water.
When my friend gave birth I held her in joy

as the child's head thrust from her vagina
like the sun rising at dawn wet and irised.

Praise our choices, sisters, for each doorway
open to us was taken by squads of fighting
women who paid years of trouble and struggle,
who paid their wombs, their sleep, their lives
that we might walk through these gates upright.
Doorways are sacred to women for we
are the doorways of life and we must choose
what comes in and what goes out. Freedom
is our real abundance.

Tumbling and with tangled mane
(COLL)

1.
I wade in milk.
Only beige sand exists as the floor
of a slender nave before me.
Mewing fishhook cries of gulls
pierce the white from what must be up.
The fog slides over me like a trained
snake leaving salt on my lips.
I can hear the ocean breathing.
The world is a benign jellyfish.
I float inhaling water that tastes
of iodine and thin bright blood.

2.

We squat on a sandbar digging as the tide
turns and runs to bury the crosshatched scales,
the ribs of the bottom as if the ebbing
of waters exposed that the world is really
a giant flounder. As we wade landward
the inrushing tide is so cold
my ankles ring like glass bells.
We lie belly up baking as the ocean
ambles toward us nibbling the sand.
Out to sea a fog bank stands like world's
end, the sharp place where boats fall off.

3.

When a storm halts, people get into their
cars. They don't start picking up yet, the bough
that crashed on the terrace, the window
shattered. No, they rush with foot hard down
on the accelerator over the wet winding black
topped roads where the pine and oak start out
normal size and get smaller till they are
forests for mice. Cars line up on the bluff
facing waves standing tall as King Kong,
skyscrapers smashed before a giant wrecking ball.
Mad water avalanches. You can't hear.
Your hair fills with wet sand. Your windshield
is being sandblasted and will blind you as the sun
burns a hole in the mist like a cigarette
through a tablecloth and sets fire to the air.

4.

A dream, two hundred times the same. The shore
can be red rocks, black or grey, sand dunes

or barrier reef. The sun blazes.
The sky roars hard, blue as policemen.
The water is kicking. The waves leap
at the shore like flames out of control.
The sea gnashes snow-capped mountains
that hurl themselves end over end, blocking
the sky. A tidal wave eats the land. Rearing
and galloping, tumbling and with tangled
mane, the horses of the surf – mad eyes,
snorting nostrils and rattling hooves –
stampede at the land. I am in danger
yet I do not run. I am rooted watching
knowing that what I watch
is also me.

Making makes guilt. Cold fierce mother
who gouges deep into this pamet, who
rests her dragon's belly on the first rocks,
older than land, older than memory,
older than life, my power is so little
it makes me laugh how in my dreaming
lemur's mind making poems or tales
is this storm on a clear day.

Of course danger and power mingle in all
birthing. We die by what we live by.
Again and again that dream comes when I set
off journeying to the back of my mind,
the bottom of the library, a joust with
what is: the sun a fiery spider high
overhead, the colors bright and clear as glass,
the sea raging at the coast, always about
to overrun it, as in the eye of a hurricane
when the waves roll cascading in undiminished
but for a moment and in that place the air

is still, the moment of clarity out
of time at the center of action.

Cutting the grapes free
(MUIN)

In spring the vine looks like a crucified
witch tied hard to high wires strung
from weathered posts. Those tormented
limbs shall never flow with sap,
dry as bones the ants have polished,
inert, resistant as obsidian.

Then from the first velvet buds tearing
open the wands stretch bouquets of skinny
serpents coiling along the wires.
Rampant swelling leaves, a dense
fluttering cascades heavy green over
the trellis and path, climbing the pine.

Now the grapes swell in the sun, yellow
and black and ruby mounds of breast
and testicle, the image of ripe flesh
rounding warm to the fingers. The wasps
and bees drone drunken, our lips, our
tongues stained purple with juice, and sweet.

We bleed when we blossom from the straight
grainy pine of girlhood. We bleed when we taste
first of men. We bleed when we bear and when
we don't. Vine, from my blood is fermented

poetry and from yours wine that tunes
my sinews and nerves till they sing.

I do not seek immortality, to be a rock
that dissolves in millennial slow motion,
but to age well like good wine harsh young
but fit to lay down, the best of me
in the dark of libraries and minds to be taken
with care into the light and savored.

I do not seek to leap free from the wheel
of change but to dance in that turning.
What depends more on the seasons
and the years than wine: whether rains come,
the pounding hail, the searing drought,
the lethal hoar kiss of the frost?

In this glass the Mosel pale as straw
shines with the sun of a spent year
and pricks my tongue with tiny bubbles
that were not there last week. The vines
of its home are blossoming and the wine
remembers its natal soil as I must.

The press of the years bears down
on us till we bleed from every pore
yet in our cells sun is stored in honey
ready to be spilled or to nurture.
Like wine I must finally trust myself
to other tongues or turn to vinegar.

The perpetual migration
(GORT)

How do we know where we are going?
How do we know where we are headed
till we in fact or hope or hunch
arrive? You can only criticize,
the comfortable say, you don't know
what you want. Ah, but we do.

We have swung in the green verandahs
of the jungle trees. We have squatted
on cloud-grey granite hillsides where
every leaf drips. We have crossed
badlands where the sun is sharp as flint.
We have paddled into the tall dark sea
in canoes. We always knew.

Peace, plenty, the gentle wallow
of intimacy, a bit of Saturday night
and not too much Monday morning,
a chance to choose, a chance to grow,
the power to say no and yes, pretties
and dignity, an occasional jolt of truth.

The brain, wrinkled slug, knows
like a computer, like a violinist, like
a bloodhound, like a frog. We remember
backwards a little and sometimes forwards,
but mostly we think in the ebbing circles
a rock makes on the water.

The salmon hurtling upstream seeks
the taste of the waters of its birth
but the seabird on its four-thousand-mile

trek follows charts mapped on its genes.
The brightness, the angle, the sighting
of the stars shines in the brain
till the inner constellation matches outer.

The stark black rocks, the island beaches
of waveworn pebbles where it will winter
look right to it. Months after it set
forth it says, home at last, and settles.
Even the pigeon beating its short whistling
wings knows the magnetic tug of arrival.

In my spine a tidal clock tilts and drips
and the moon pulls blood from my womb.
Driven as a migrating falcon, I can be blown
off course yet if I turn back, it feels
wrong. Navigating by chart and chance
and passion, I will know the shape
of the mountains of freedom, I will know.

The great horned owl
(NGETAL)

I wake after midnight and hear
you hunting: that sound seems to lodge
in the nape like a hollow bullet,
a rhythmic hooting plaintive as if
you seduced your prey by pity.

How you swoop from the dark of the trees
against the blackest blue sky of the November
full moon, your wings spread wide as my
arms, rough heavy sails rigged for a storm.

The moon blinds me as she glides in ripping
skeins of cloud. On your forehead you bear
her crescents, your eyes hypnotic
as her clock-face disc. Gale force winds
strip crispened leaves from the branches
and try the strength of the wood. The weakest
die now, giving back their bodies
for the white sheet of the snow to cover.

Now my cats are not let out after sunset
because you own the night. I fear and protect
you, come to harry the weak in the long dark.
Pellets of mouse and bird and shrew bone
I will find at the base of the pines.
You have come to claim your nest again
in the old white oak whose heart is thick
with age, and in the dead of the winter
when the snow has wept into ice and frozen
and been buried again in snow and crusted over,
you will give birth before the willow buds
swell and all night you will hunt for those
first babies of the year, downy owlets shivering.
Waking to hear you I touch the warm back
of my lover sleeping beside me on his stomach
like a child.

The longest night
(RUIS)

The longest night is long drawn
as a freight blocking a grade crossing
in a prairie town when I am trying
to reach Kansas City to sleep and one
boxcar clatters after the other, after
and after in faded paint proclaiming
as they trundle through the headlights
names of 19th-century fortunes, scandals,
labor wars. Stalled between factory
and cemetery I lean on the cold wheel.
The factory is still, the machines
turned off; the cemetery looks boring
and factual as a parking lot. Too cold
for the dead to stir, tonight even
my own feel fragile as brown bags
carted to the dump. Ash stains the air.
Wheels of the freight clack by. Snow
hisses on the windshield of the rented car.
Always a storm at the winter solstice.

New moon, no moon, old moon dying,
moon that gives no light, stub
of a candle, dark lantern, face
without features, the zone of zero:
I feel my weakness summoning me
like a bed of soft grey ashes
I might crawl into.

Here in the pit of the year scars overlap
scabs, the craters of the moon, stone
breaking stone. In the rearview mirror

my black hair fades into the night,
my cheeks look skeletal, my dark eyes,
holes a rat might hide in. I sense
death lurking up the road like a feral
dog abroad in the swirling snow.

Defeat, defeat, defeat, tedious
as modern headstones, regular as dentures.
My blood tastes salty as tears and rusty
as an old nail. Yet as I kick the car
over the icy tracks toward nowhere
I want to be, I am grinning. Lady, it's been
worse before, bad as the moon burning,
bad as the moon's horn goring my side,
that to give up now is a joke told
by the FBI minding the tap or the binoculars
staking me out on such a bitter night
when the blood slows and begins to freeze.
I grew up among these smoke-pitted houses
choking over the railroad between the factory
shuddering and the cemetery for the urban
poor, and I got out. They say that's
what you ask for. And how much more
I ask. To get everybody out.

Hecate, lady of the crossroads, vampires
of despair you loose and the twittering
bats of sleepless fear. The three-headed
dog barking in the snow obeys you.
Tonight I honor you, lady of last things.
Without you to goad me I would lie
late in the warm bed of the flesh.
The blood I coughed from my lungs that year
you stood at the foot of my bed was sour,
acrid, the taste of promises broken

and since then I have run twice as fast.
Your teeth are in me, like tiny headstones.
This moon is the void around which the serpent
with its tail in its mouth curls.
Where there is no color, no light,
no sound, what is? The dark of the mind.
In terror begins vision. In silence
I learn my song, here at the stone
nipple, the black moon bleeding,
the egg anonymous as water,
the night that goes on and on,
a tunnel through the earth.

At the well
(BETH)

Though I'm blind now and age
has gutted me to rubbing bones
knotted up in a leather sack
like Old Man Jacob I wrestled an angel.
It happened near that well by Peniel
where the water runs copper cold
even in drought. Sore and dusty
I was traveling my usual rounds
wary of strangers, for some men
think nothing of setting on any woman
alone, doctoring a bit, setting bones,
herbs and simples I know well,
divining for water with a switch,
selling my charms of odd shaped bones
and stones with fancy names to less

skeptical women wanting a lover, a son,
a husband, or relief from one.

The stones were sharp as shinbones under me.
When I woke up at midnight it had come,
not he, I thought, not she but a presence furious
as a goat about to butt.
Amused as those yellow eyes
sometimes seem just before the hind
legs kick hard.
The angel struck me
and we wrestled all that night.
My dust-stained gristle of a body
clad in proper village black
was pushed against him
and his fiery chest
fell through me like a star.
Raw with bruises, with my muscles
sawing like donkey's brays,
I thought fighting can be
making love. Then in the grey
placental dawn I saw.

'I know you now, face
on a tree of fire
with eyes of my youngest sweetest
dead, face
I saw in the mirror
right after my first child
was born – before it failed –
when I was beautiful.
Whatever you are, whatever
I've won a blessing
from you. Bless me!'

The angel, 'Yes, we have met
at doors thrust open to an empty room,

a garden, or a pit.
My gifts have human faces
hieroglyphs that command
you without yielding what they mean.
Cast yourself
and I will bless your cast
till your bones are dice
for the wind to roll.
I am the demon of beginnings
for those who leap their thresholds
and let the doors swing shut.'

My hair bristling, I stood.
'Get away from me, old
enemy. I know the lying
radiance of that face:
my friend, my twin, my
lover I trusted as the fish
the water, who left me
carrying his child.
The man who bought me
with his strength and beat
me for his weakness.
The girl I saved who turned
and sold her skin
for an easy bed in a house
of slaves. The boy fresh
as a willow sapling
smashed on the stones of war.'

'I am the spirit of hinges,
the fever that lives in dice
and cards, what is picked
up and thrown down. I am
the new that is ancient,
the hope that hurts,

what begins in what has ended.
Mine is the double vision
that everything is sacred, and trivial,
the laughter that bubbles in blood,
and I love the blue beetle
clicking in the grass as much
as you. Shall I bless you,
child and crone?'

'What has plucked the glossy
pride of hair from my scalp,
loosened my teeth in their sockets,
wrung my breasts dry as gullies,
rubbed ashes into my sleep
but chasing you?
Now I clutch a crust and I hold on.
Get from me,
wielder of the heart's mirages.
I will follow you to no more graves.'

I spat
and she gathered her tall shuddering wings
and scaled the streaks of the dawn
a hawk on fire soaring
and I stood there and could hear the water burbling
and raised my hand
before my face and groped:
Why has the sun gone out?
Why is it dark?

White on black

(LUIS)

They say the year begins in January, but it
feels like the same old year to me. Things
give out now, the cabbages rot, the rent
in the coat sleeve's too worn to be mended,
the boot finally admits it leaks, the candle
nub gutters out with a banner of pungent smoke.

The cracked dish of the frozen moon lights
the snow far longer than the old fox of the sun
that can hardly scale the hill, that crawls
feebly into the lower branches of the pine
and drops to earth exhausted.

                                    Little sister
of the moon you prance on the ice with
delicate black feet. Your eyes shine red.
You comb your long tail and plume it out.
You mate under the porch. With sharp claws
you dig up the compost and scavenge the dump.
The air is crystal up to the ice splinters
of stars but you raise the quickest warm
nose in the woods, long, sharp as your hunger.

In the path you wait for me to give way.
Often you die bloody in the road because
you expect deference. The wise dog looks
the other way when you cross his yard.
The stupid dog never bothers you twice.

Little sister, mostly when we meet we bow
rather formally and go our ways, me
first. I read in a book that perhaps if one
lifted you by your tail, you could not spray
or perhaps you could. I envision a man

[234]

in a space suit lumbering over the plain
of the Herring River to catch and lift
you in the name of science. Then the space
suit would be burned perhaps or perhaps
not. My cats and I sit in the darkened
livingroom watching through the glass
as you dance and nibble, your long fur
sweeping the snow and your nailed feet quick.

Another country
(NION)

When I visited with the porpoises
I felt awkward, my hairy
angular body sprouting its skinny
grasping limbs like long mistakes.
The child of gravity and want I sank
in the salt wave clattering with gadgets,
appendages. Millennia past
they turned and fled back to the womb.
There they feel no fatigue but slip
through the water caressed and buoyed up.
Never do they sleep but their huge brains
hold life always turning it like a pebble
under the tongue, and lacking practice, death
comes as an astonishment.

In the wide murmur of the sea they fear
little. Together they ram the shark.
Food swims flashing in schools.
Hunger is only a teasing, endured
no longer than desired. Weather

is superficial decoration; they rise
to salute the thunder, romping their tails.

They ride through pleasure and plenty
secure in a vast courtesy
firm enough to sustain a drowning man.
Nothing is said bluntly.
All conversation is a singing,
all telling alludes to and embodies
minute displacements in epic,
counter-epic, comic opera, or the four hundred
forty-one other genres they recognize
as current. Every exchange comes
as aria, lyric, set piece, recitativo,
and even a cry for help is couched
in a form brief and terse,
strict as haiku.

Greed has no meaning when no one
is hungry. Thus they swim toward
us with broad grins and are slaughtered
by the factory ships
that harvest the tuna like wheat.

Crescent moon like a canoe
(FEARN)

This month you carried me late and heavy
in your belly and finally near Tuesday
midnight you gave me light and life, the season
Kore returns to Demeter, and you suffer
and I cannot save you though I burn with dreams.

Memories the color of old blood,
scraps of velvet gowns, lace, chiffon veils,
your sister's stage costumes (Ziegfeld
didn't stint) we fingered together, you
padding in sneakers and wash-worn housedresses.

You grew celery by tucking sliced off
bottoms in the soil. You kept a compost
pile in 1940. Your tomatoes glowed
like traffic signals in the table-sized yard.
Don't kill spiders, you warned.

In an asbestos box in Detroit where sputtering
factories yellow the air, where sheets
on the line turn ashen, you nurtured
a backyard jungle. Every hungry cat
wanted to enter and every child.

You who had not been allowed to finish
tenth grade but sent to be a frightened
chambermaid, carried home every week
armloads of books from the library
rummaging them late at night, insomniac,

riffling the books like boxes of chocolates
searching for the candied cherries, the nuts,
hunting for the secrets, the formulae,

the knowledge those others learned
that made them shine and never ache.

You were taught to feel stupid; you
were made to feel dirty; you were
forced to feel helpless; you were trained
to feel lost, uprooted, terrified.
You could not love yourself or me.

Dreamer of fables that hid their own
endings, kitchen witch, reader of palms,
you gave me gifts and took them back
but the real ones boil in the blood
and swell in the breasts, furtive, strong.

You gave me hands that can pick up
a wild bird so that the bird relaxes,
turns and stares. I have handled
fifty stunned and injured birds and killed
only two through clumsiness, with your touch.

You taught me to see the scale on the bird
leg, the old woman's scalp pink as a rose
under the fluff, the golden flecks in the iris
of your eye, the silver underside of leaves
blown back. I am your poet, mother.

You did not want the daughter you got.
You wanted a girl to flirt as you did
and marry as you had and chew the same
sour coughed up cud, yet you wanted too
to birth a witch, a revenger, a sword

of hearts who would do all the things
you feared. Don't do it, they'll kill
you, you're bad, you said, slapping me down
hard but always you whispered, I could have!
Only rebellion flashes like lightning.

I wanted to take you with me, you don't
remember. We fought like snakes, biting
hard at each other's spine to snap free.
You burned my paper armor, rifled my diaries,
snuffed my panties looking for smudge of sex,

so I took off and never came back. You can't
imagine how I still long to save you,
to carry you off, who can't trust me
to make coffee, but your life and mine pass
in different centuries, under altered suns.

I see your blood soaking into the linoleum,
I see you twisted, a mop some giant hand
is wringing out. Pain in the careless joke
and shouted insult and knotted fist. Pain like knives
and forks set out on the domestic table.

You look to men for salvation and every year
finds you more helpless. Do I battle
for other women, myself included,
because I cannot give you anything
you want? I cannot midwife you free.

In my childhood bed we float, your sweet
husky voice singing about the crescent
moon, with two horns sharp and bright we would
climb into like a boat and row away
and see, you sang, where the pretty moon goes.

In the land where the moon hides, mothers
and daughters hold each other tenderly.
There is no male law at five o'clock.
Our sameness and our difference do not clash
metal on metal but we celebrate and learn.

My muse, your voice on the phone wavers with tears.
The life you gave me burns its acetylene

of buried anger, unused talents, rotted wishes,
the compost of discontent, flaring into words
strong for other women under your waning moon.

O!

Oh, the golden bauble of your rising
wet from the waves rippling,
radiating like orgasm, round
as a singing mouth at full stretch,
round as the vagina when it takes,
round as a full belly, round
as a baby's head, you come to us
riding over the white manes
of the waves, walking on their backs
like a circus rider. Hoop
of cool fire, goose egg,
silver mirror in which we see
ourselves dimly but truly reflected,
our blood is salty water
you tug at, drawing us.
Red onion, I peel you layer
by layer and weep. The nights
carve you and then you swell
again, lady of the wild animals
whose homes are paved and poisoned,
lady of the furry mammals at teat
and the shimmering fish whose sides
echo you, of those who hunt for roots
and berries, hunt for the island
in the sea where love rules and women

are free to wax and wane and wander
in the sweet strict seasons
of our desires and needs.

IN THE TEMPLE OF THE DIASPORA

The ram's horn sounding

1.
Giant porcupine, I walk a rope braided
of my intestines and veins, beige and blue and red,
while clutched in my arms, you lie glaring
sore eyed, snuffling and sticking your spines at me.

Always I am finding quills worked into some unsuspected
muscle, an innocent pillow of fat pierced by you.
We sleep in the same bed nightly and you take it all.
I wake shuddering with cold, the quilt stripped from me.

No, not a porcupine: a leopard cub.
Beautiful you are as light and as darkness.
Avid, fierce, demanding with sharp teeth
to be fed and tended, you only want my life.

Ancient, living, a deep and tortuous river
that rose in the stark mountains beyond the desert,
you have gouged through rocks with slow persistence
enduring, meandering in long shining coils to the sea.

2.
A friend who had been close before being recruited
by the CIA once sent me a postcard of the ghetto at Tetuan
yellowed like old pornography, numbered 17,
a prime number as one might say a prime suspect.

The photographer stood well clear of the gate
to shoot old clothes tottering in the tight street,
beards matted and holy with grease,
children crooked under water jugs,

old men austere and busy as hornets.
Flies swarmed on the lens.
Dirt was the color.

Oh, I understood your challenge.
My Jewishness seemed to you sentimental,
perverse, planned obsolescence.
Paris was hot and dirty the night I first
met relatives who had survived the war.
My identity squatted whining on my arm
gorging itself on my thin blood.
A gaggle of fierce insistent speakers of ten
languages had different passports mother
from son, brother from sister, had four
passports all forged, kept passports
from gone countries (Transylvania, Bohemia,
old despotisms fading like Victorian wallpaper),
were used to sewing contraband into coat
linings. I smuggled for them across two borders.
Their wars were old ones.
Mine was just starting.

Sharp debater, it's easy in any manscape
to tell the haves from the have-nots.
Any ghetto is a kleinbottle.
You think you are outside gazing idly in.
Winners write history; losers
die of it, like the plague.

3.
A woman and a Jew, sometimes more
of a contradiction than I can sweat out,
yet finally the intersection that is both
collision and fusion, stone and seed.

Like any poet I wrestle the holy name
and know there is no wording finally
can map, constrain or summon that fierce
voice whose long wind lifts my hair

chills my skin and fills my lungs
to bursting. I serve the word
I cannot name, who names me daily,
who speaks me out by whispers and shouts.

Coming to the new year, I am picked
up like the ancient ram's horn to sound
over the congregation of people and beetles,
of pines, whales, marshhawks and asters.

Then I am dropped into the factory of words
to turn my little wheels and grind my own
edges, back on piece work again, knowing
there is no justice we don't make daily

like bread and love. Shekinah,
stooping on hawk wings prying into my heart
with your silver beak; floating down
a milkweed silk dove of sunset;

riding the filmy sheets of rain like a ghost
ship with all sails still unfurled;
bless me and use me for telling and naming
the forever collapsing shades and shapes of life,

the rainbows cast across our eyes by the moment
of sun, the shadows we trail across the grass
running, the opal valleys of the night flesh,
the moments of knowledge ripping into the brain

and aligning everything into a new pattern
as a constellation learned organizes blur

into stars; our blood kinship with all green, hairy
and scaled folk born from the ancient warm sea.

Nishmat

When the night slides under with the last dimming star
and the red sky lightens between the trees,
and the heron glides tipping heavy wings in the river,
when crows stir and cry out their harsh joy,
and swift creatures of the night run toward their burrows,
and the deer raises her head and sniffs the freshening air,
and the shadows grow more distinct and then shorten,

then we rise into the day still clean as new snow.
The cat washes its paw and greets the day with gratitude.
Leviathan salutes breaching with a column of steam.
The hawk turning in the sky cries out a prayer like a knife.
We must wonder at the sky now thin as a speckled eggshell,
that now piles up its boulders of storm to crash down,
that now hangs a furry grey belly into the street.

Every day we find a new sky and a new earth
with which we are trusted like a perfect toy.
We are given the salty river of our blood
winding through us, to remember the sea and our
kindred under the waves, the hot pulsing that knocks
in our throats to consider our cousins in the grass
and the trees, all bright scattered rivulets of life.

We are given the wind within us, the breath
to shape into words that steal time, that touch
like hands and pierce like bullets, that waken
truth and deceit, sorrow and pity and joy,

that waste precious air in complaints, in lies,
in floating traps for power on the dirty air.
Yet holy breath still stretches our lungs to sing.

We are given the body, that momentary kibbutz
of elements that have belonged to frog and polar
bear, corn and oak tree, volcano and glacier.
We are lent for a time these minerals in water
and a morning every day, a morning to wake up,
rejoice and praise life in our spines, our throats,
our knees, our genitals, our brains, our tongues.

We are given fire to see against the dark,
to think, to read, to study how we are to live,
to bank in ourselves against defeat and despair
that cool and muddy our resolves, that make us forget
what we saw we must do. We are given passion
to rise like the sun in our minds with the new day
and burn the debris of habit and greed and fear.

We stand in the midst of the burning world
primed to burn with compassionate love and justice,
to turn inward and find holy fire at the core,
to turn outward and see the world that is all
of one flesh with us, see under the trash, through
the smog, the furry bee in the apple blossom,
the trout leaping, the candles our ancestors lit for us.

Fill us as the tide rustles into the reeds in the marsh.
Fill us as the rushing water overflows the pitcher.
Fill us as light fills a room with its dancing.
Let the little quarrels of the bones and the snarling
of the lesser appetites and the whining of the ego cease.
Let silence still us so you may show us your shining
and we can out of that stillness rise and praise.

The housing project at Drancy

Trains without signs flee through Paris.
Wrong trains. The wrong station.
The world as microwave oven, burning from within.
We arrive. Drancy looks like Inkster,
Gary, the farther reaches of Newark.

In the station they won't give directions.
C'est pas notre affaire. We don't deal with that.
Outside five buses limp in five directions
into the hot plain drugged with exhaust.
Nobody ever heard of the camp. They turn away.

Out on the bridge, over marshalling yards:
Here Jews were stuffed into cars nailed shut.
Here children too young to know their names
were counted like so many shoes
as they begged the French police hemming them in,

Take me to the bathroom, please, please,
before I wet myself. Mother, I have been so good,
and it is so very dark. Dear concierge,
I am writing to you as everyone else
is dead now and they are taking me away.

Yes, to the land children named Pichepois,
giant's skull land grimmer than Hansel came to.
On the bridge I saw an old bald workman
staring down and I told myself desperately,
He is a communist and will answer me.

I asked him where the camp was, now a housing
project. He asked, Why do you want to know?
I had that one ready. No talk of novels, research.
My aunt was there. Oh, in that case,
he pointed to distant towers. You want that bus.

Where we descended the bus, Never heard of it.
Eyes that won't look. Then a woman asked that
same question, Why do you want to know?
A housing project crammed with mothers.
The guard towers are torn down and lindens grow.

In flats now with heat and plumbing, not eighty
but one family lives. Pain still rises,
the groaning of machinery deep underfoot.
Crimes ignored sink into the soil like PCBs
and enter the bones of children.

Black Mountain

On Montagne Noire creeping everywhere under the beech trees
were immense black slugs the size and pattern
of blown truck tires exploded by the superhighway.
Diamonds patterned their glossy and glittering backs.

As we watched, leaves, whole flowers disappeared in three bites.
Such avidity rebuked our stomachs skittish with alien
water and strange food. In patches of sunlight filtered
down, the slugs shone like wet black glass.

Battlefields are like any other fields; a forest
where men and women fought tanks with sten guns
houses as many owl and rabbit and deer as the next hill
where nothing's happened since the Romans passed by.

Yet I have come without hesitation through the maze
of lumbering roads to this spot where the small marker
tells us we have reached a destination. To die here
under hemlock's dark drooping boughs, better I think

than shoved into the showers of gas to croak like roaches
too packed in to flail in the intense slow pain
as the minutes like lava cooling petrified the jammed
bodies into living rock, basalt pillars whose fingers

gouged grooves in cement. Yes, better to drop in the high
clean air and let your blood soak into the rich leaf mold.
Better to get off one good shot. Better to remember trains
derailed, turntables wrecked with plastique, raids

on the munitions dump. Better to die with a gun
in your hand you chose to pick up and had time to shoot.
Dying you pass out of choice. The others come, put up
a monument decorated with crosses, no Mogen Davids.

I come avid and omnivorous as the shining slugs.
I have eaten your history and made it myth;
among the tall trees of your pain my characters walk.
A saw whines in the valley. I say kaddish for you.

Blessed only is the act. The act of defiance,
the act of justice that fills the mouth with blood.
Blessed is the act of survival that saves the blood.
Blessed is the act of art that paints the blood

redder than real and quicker, that restores
the fallen tree to its height and birds. Memory
is the simplest form of prayer. Today you glow
like warm precious lumps of amber in my mind.

Returning to the cemetery in the old Prague ghetto

Like bad teeth jammed crooked in a mouth
I think, no, because it goes on and on,
rippling among uneven hillocks among the linden
trees drooping, their papery leaves piling
up in the narrow paths that thread
between the crowded tilting slabs.

Stone pages the wind blew open.
The wind petrified into individual
cries. Prisoners penned together
with barely room to stand upright.
Souls of the dead Jews of Prague
waiting for justice under the acid rain.

So much and no further shall you go,
your contaminated dead confined between
strait walls like the ghetto itself.
So what to do? Every couple of generations,
pile on the dirt, raise the stones up
and add another layer of fresh bones.

The image I circle and do not want:
naked pallid bodies whipped through
the snow and driven into the chamber,
so crowded that dying slowly in the poison
cloud they could not fall as their nerves
burned slowly black, upright in death.

In my luggage I carried from Newcomb Hollow
two stones for Rabbi Loew's memorial
shaped like a narrow tent, one for Judah

on his side and one for Perl on hers.
But my real gift is the novel they
speak through. For David Gans, astronomer,

geographer, historian, insatiably curious
and neat as a cat in his queries,
I brought a fossil to lay at the foot
of his grave marked with a goose and a star,
Mogen David, so the illiterate could find
him, as Judah has his rampant lion.

In sixty-eight I had to be hoisted
over the fence. Among the stones
I was alone except for a stray black cat
that sang to me incessantly of need,
so hungry it ate bread from my jacket pocket.
This year buses belch out German tourists

and the graves are well tended.
This is a place history clutches you
by the foot as you walk the human earth,
like a hand grabbing from the grave,
not to frighten but to admonish.
Remember. History is the iron

in your blood carrying oxygen
so you can burn food and live.
Read this carved book with your fingers
and your failing eyes. The language
will speak in you silently
nights afterward, stone and bone.

My rich uncle, whom I only met three times

We were never invited to his house.
We went there once while they were all in Hawaii,
climbed steps from which someone had shoveled
the snow, not him, to the wide terrace.
Yellow brick, the house peered into fir and juniper.
It was too large for me to imagine what it held
but I was sure everyone of them, four girls
and bony wife, each had a room of her own.

He had been a magician and on those rare
nights he had to stay at the Detroit Statler
downtown, he would summon us for supper
in the hotel restaurant. Mother would put on
and take off every dress in her closet, all six,
climb in the swaybacked brown Hudson muttering shame.
He would do tricks with his napkin and pull
quarters from my ears and spoons from his sleeves.

He had been a clumsy acrobat, he had failed at comedy
and vaudeville; he was entertaining for a party
when he met a widow with four girls and an inheritance.
He waltzed right out of her romantic movie dreams
and he strolled into her house and she had him redone.
He learned to talk almost like her dead husband.
He learned to wear suits, order dinners and give orders
to servants. His name changed, his background rebuilt,
his religion painted over, he almost fit in.

Of my uncles, only he was unreal, arriving by plane
to stay on the fanciest street in downtown Detroit.
The waiter brought a phone to the table, his broker

calling. I imagined a cowboy breaking horses.
He made knives disappear. He made a napkin vanish.
He was like an animated suit, no flesh, no emotions
bubbling the blood and steaming the windows
as my other uncles and aunts did. Only the discrete
Persian leather smell of money droned in my nose.

His longest trick was to render himself invisible.
Then one night after the guests had left, he went down
to the basement in the latest multi-level glass vast
whatnot shelf of house and hanged himself by the furnace.
They did not want his family at the funeral. She had
no idea, his wife said, why would he be depressed?
I remember his laugh like a cough and his varnished
face, buffed till the silverware shone in his eyes.
His last trick was to vanish himself forever.

After the wind abated, he walked out and died

(*for Arne Manos 1941–1991*)

A little green snake trapped
like a silken braid
in the hands, quick jerk
of the supple spine
and it glides free
gone into the camouflage grass.

Blue eyes of the dayflower
weed among the alyssum
like the hemerocallis
opens each day its fresh flower

that fades and withers
with the bleeding sun.

I would have eaten more chocolate
if I'd known said the dying
woman, I would have told all
my affection, I would have lain
reading the worry beads of his spine
an hour to each.

But we do know.
The clock face opens and
closes its scissor hands
cutting us from the minute
the hour that never
comes back.

The watch in our chest keeps
time for us – keeps? No,
spends the time as it runs through
us on its millipede legs.
This is our longest dance, but we
lose the patterns we are casting.

We die always in the moment
like a book falling shut
and the story is finished except
for those resonances that darken
in the minds of others, toward silence
and the long cold between the stars.

Kaddish

Look around us, search above us, below, behind.
We stand in a great web of being joined together.
Let us praise, let us love the life we are lent
passing through us in the body of Israel
and our own bodies, let's say amen.

Time flows through us like water.
The past and the dead speak through us.
We breathe out our children's children, blessing.

Blessed is the earth from which we grow,
blessed the life we are lent,
blessed the ones who teach us,
blessed the ones we teach,
blessed is the word that cannot say the glory
that shines through us and remains to shine
flowing past distant suns on the way to forever.
Let's say amen.

Blessed is light, blessed is darkness,
but blessed above all else is peace
which bears the fruits of knowledge
on strong branches, let's say amen.

Peace that bears joy into the world,
peace that enables love, peace over Israel
everywhere, blessed and holy is peace, let's say amen.

The Book of Ruth and Naomi

When you pick up the Tanakh and read
the Book of Ruth, it is a shock
how little it resembles memory.
It's concerned with inheritance,
lands, men's names, how women
must wiggle and wobble to live.

Yet women have kept it dear
for the beloved elder who
cherished Ruth, more friend than
daughter. Daughters leave. Ruth
brought even the baby she made
with Boaz home as a gift.

Where you go, I will go too,
your people shall be my people,
I will be a Jew for you,
for what is yours I will love
as I love you, oh Naomi
my mother, my sister, my heart.

Show me a woman who does not dream
a double, heart's twin, a sister
of the mind in whose ear she can whisper,
whose hair she can braid as her life
twists its pleasure and pain and shame.
Show me a woman who does not hide

in the locket of bone that deep
eye beam of fiercely gentle love
she had once from mother, daughter,
sister; once like a warm moon

that radiance aligned the tides
of her blood into potent order.

At the season of first fruits we remember
those travellers, co-conspirators, scavengers
making do with leftovers and mill ends,
whose friendship was stronger than fear,
stronger than hunger, who walked together
down death's dusty road, hands joined.

Maggid

The courage to let go of the door, the handle.
The courage to shed the familiar walls whose very
stains and leaks are comfortable as the little moles
of the upper arm; stains that recall a feast,
a child's naughtiness, a loud blattering storm
that slapped the roof hard, pouring through.

The courage to abandon the graves dug into the hill,
the small bones of children and the brittle bones
of the old whose marrow hunger had stolen;
the courage to desert the tree planted and only
begun to bear; the riverside where promises were
shaped; the street where their empty pots were broken.

The courage to leave the place whose language you learned
as early as your own, whose customs however dan-
gerous or demeaning, bind you like a halter
you have learned to pull inside, to move your load;
the land fertile with the blood spilled on it;
the roads mapped and annotated for survival.

The courage to walk out of the pain that is known
into the pain that cannot be imagined,
mapless, walking into the wilderness, going
barefoot with a canteen into the desert;
stuffed in the stinking hold of a rotting ship
sailing off the map into dragons' mouths,

Cathay, India, Siberia, goldeneh medina,
leaving bodies by the way like abandoned treasure.
So they walked out of Egypt. So they bribed their way
out of Russia under loads of straw; so they steamed
out of the bloody smoking charnelhouse of Europe
on overloaded freighters forbidden all ports –

out of pain into death or freedom or a different
painful dignity, into squalor and politics.
We Jews are all born of wanderers, with shoes
under our pillows and a memory of blood that is ours
raining down. We honor only those Jews who changed
tonight, those who chose the desert over bondage

who walked into the strange and became strangers
and gave birth to children who could look down
on them standing on their shoulders for having
been slaves. We honor those who let go of everything but freedom, who ran, who revolted, who fought,
who became other by saving themselves.

For she is a tree of life

In the cramped living room of my childhood
between sagging rough-skinned sofa that made me itch
and swaybacked chair surrounded by ashtrays
where my father read every word of the paper
shrouded in blue smoke, coughing rusty phlegm
and muttering doom, the rug was a factory
oriental and the pattern called tree of life.

My mother explained as we plucked a chicken,
tree of life: I was enthralled and Hannah
my grandmother hummed for me the phrase
from liturgy: Eytz khayim hee l'makhazikim
bo v'kol nitee-voteh-ho shalom:
for she is a tree of life to all who hold her fast,
and the fruit of her branches is peace.

I see her big bosomed and tall as a maple
and in her veins the beige sugar of desire
running sometimes hard, surging skyward
and sometimes sunk down into the roots
that burrow and wriggle deep and far among rocks
and clay and the bones of rabbits and foxes
lying in the same bed at last becoming one.

I see her opening into flushed white
blossoms the bees crawl into, I see her
branches dipping under the weight of fruit,
the crimson, the yellow and russet apples,
fruit fallen beneath the deer crunch,
yellow jackets in the cobalt afternoon buzzing
drunken from cracked fruit oozing juice.

All living flit through her branches or creep
through her bark, skitter over her leaves.
Yet we ourselves are the mice that gnaw at her root
who labor ceaselessly to bring her down.
When the tree falls, we will not rise as plastic
ballpoint spaceships, but will starve as the skies
weep hot acid and the earth chafes into dust.

Coming up on September

White butterflies, with single
black fingerpaint eyes on their wings
dart and settle, eddy and mate
over the green tangle of vines
in Labor Day morning steam.

The year grinds into ripeness
and rot, grapes darkening,
pears yellowing, the first
Virginia creeper twining crimson,
the grasses, dry straw to burn.

The New Year rises, beckoning
across the umbrellas on the sand.
I begin to reconsider my life.
What is the yield of my impatience?
What is the fruit of my resolve?

I turn from my frantic white dance
over the jungle of productivity
and slowly a niggun slides,

cold water down my throat.
I rest on a leaf spotted red.

Now is the time to let the mind
search backwards like the raven loosed
to see what can feed us. Now,
the time to cast the mind forward
to chart an aerial map of the months.

The New Year is a great door
that stands across the evening and Yom
Kippur is the second door. Between them
are song and silence, stone and clay pot
to be filled from within myself.

I will find there both ripeness and rot,
what I have done and undone,
what I must let go with the waning days
and what I must take in. With the last
tomatoes, we harvest the fruit of our lives.

Breadcrumbs

Some time on Rosh Hashana I go,
a time dictated by tide charts,
services. The once I did tashlich

on the rising tide and the crumbs
floated back to me, my energy soured,
vinegar of anxiety. Now I eye the times.

I choose the dike, where the Herring River
pours in and out of the bay, where at
low tide in September blue herons stalk

totemic to spear the alewives hastening
silver-sided from the fresh ponds to
the sea. As I toss my crumbs, muttering

prayers, a fisherman rebukes me: It's
not right to feed the fish, it distracts
them from his bait. Sometimes

it's odd to be a Jew, like a three-
legged heron with bright purple head,
an ibis in white plumes diving

except that with global warming
we do sometimes glimpse an ibis
in our marshes, and I am rooted here

to abide the winter when this tourist
has gone back to Cincinnati.
My rituals are mated to this fawn

colored land floating on the horizon
of water. My havurah calls itself
Am ha-Yam, people of the sea,

and we are wedded to the oceans
as truly as the Venetian doge who tossed
his gold ring to the Adriatic.

All rivers flow at last into the sea
but here it is, at once. So we stand
the tourist casting for his fish

and I tossing my bread. The fish
snap it up. Tonight perhaps
he will broil my sins for supper.

The task never completed

No task is ever completed,
only abandoned or pressed into use.
Tinkering can be a form of prayer.

Twenty-six botched worlds preceded
Genesis we are told in ancient commentary,
and ha Shem said not only,

of this particular attempt
It is good, but muttered,
if only it will hold.

Incomplete, becoming, the world
was given us to fix, to complete
and we've almost worn it out.

My house was hastily built,
on the cheap. Leaks, rotting
sills, the floor a relief map of Idaho.

Whenever I get some money, I stove
up, repair, add on, replace.
This improvisation permits me to squat

here on the land that owns me.
We evolve through mistakes, wrong
genes, imitation gone wild.

Each night sleep unravels me into wool,
then into sheep and wolf. Walls and fire
pass through me. I birth stones.

Every dawn I stumble from the roaring
vat of dreams and make myself up
remembering and forgetting by halves.

Every dawn I choose to take a knife
to the world's flank or a sewing kit,
rough improvisation, but a start.

The art of blessing the day

This is the blessing for rain after drought:
Come down, wash the air so it shimmers,
a perfumed shawl of lavender chiffon.
Let the parched leaves suckle and swell.
Enter my skin, wash me for the little
chrysalis of sleep rocked in your plashing.
In the morning the world is peeled to shining.

This is the blessing for sun after long rain:
Now everything shakes itself free and rises.
The trees are bright as pushcart ices.
Every last lily opens its satin thighs.
The bees dance and roll in pollen
and the cardinal at the top of the pine
sings at full throttle, fountaining.

This is the blessing for a ripe peach:
This is luck made round. Frost can nip
the blossom, kill the bee. It can drop,
a hard green useless nut. Brown fungus,
the burrowing worm that coils in rot can
blemish it and wind crush it on the ground.
Yet this peach fills my mouth with juicy sun.

This is the blessing for the first garden tomato:
Those green boxes of tasteless acid the store
sells in January, those red things with the savor

of wet chalk, they mock your fragrant name.
How fat and sweet you are weighing down my palm,
warm as the flank of the cow in the sun.
You are the savor of summer in a thin red skin.

This is the blessing for a political victory:
Although I shall not forget that things
work in increments and epicycles and sometime
leaps that half the time fall back down,
let's not relinquish dancing while the music
fits into our hips and bounces our heels.
We must never forget, pleasure is real as pain.

The blessing for the return of a favorite cat,
the blessing for love returned, for friends'
return, for money received unexpected,
the blessing for the rising of the bread,
the sun, the oppressed. I am not sentimental
about old men mumbling the Hebrew by rote
with no more feeling than one says gesundheit.

But the discipline of blessings is to taste
each moment, the bitter, the sour, the sweet
and the salty, and be glad for what does not
hurt. The art is in compressing attention
to each little and big blossom of the tree
of life, to let the tongue sing each fruit,
its savor, its aroma and its use.

Attention is love, what we must give
children, mothers, fathers, pets,
our friends, the news, the woes of others.
What we want to change we curse and then
pick up a tool. Bless whatever you can
with eyes and hands and tongue. If you
can't bless it, get ready to make it new.

Index of Titles

Index of First Lines

Discover more about our forthcoming books through Penguin's FREE newspaper...

Penguin
Quarterly

It's packed with:

- exciting features

- author interviews

- previews & reviews

- books from your favourite
  films & TV series

- exclusive competitions
  & much, much more...

Write off for your free copy today to:
Dept JC
Penguin Books Ltd
FREEPOST
West Drayton
Middlesex
UB7 0BR
NO STAMP REQUIRED

READ MORE IN PENGUIN

In every corner of the world, on every subject under the sun, Penguin represents quality and variety – the very best in publishing today.

For complete information about books available from Penguin – including Puffins, Penguin Classics and Arkana – and how to order them, write to us at the appropriate address below. Please note that for copyright reasons the selection of books varies from country to country.

In the United Kingdom: Please write to *Dept. JC, Penguin Books Ltd, FREEPOST, West Drayton, Middlesex UB7 OBR.*

If you have any difficulty in obtaining a title, please send your order with the correct money, plus ten per cent for postage and packaging, to *PO Box No. 11, West Drayton, Middlesex UB7 OBR*

In the United States: Please write to *Consumer Sales, Penguin USA, P.O. Box 999, Dept. 17109, Bergenfield, New Jersey 07621-0120.* VISA and MasterCard holders call 1-800-253-6476 to order all Penguin titles

In Canada: Please write to *Penguin Books Canada Ltd, 10 Alcorn Avenue, Suite 300, Toronto, Ontario M4V 3B2*

In Australia: Please write to *Penguin Books Australia Ltd, P.O. Box 257, Ringwood, Victoria 3134*

In New Zealand: Please write to *Penguin Books (NZ) Ltd, Private Bag 102902, North Shore Mail Centre, Auckland 10*

In India: Please write to *Penguin Books India Pvt Ltd, 706 Eros Apartments, 56 Nehru Place, New Delhi 110 019*

In the Netherlands: Please write to *Penguin Books Netherlands bv, Postbus 3507, NL-1001 AH Amsterdam*

In Germany: Please write to *Penguin Books Deutschland GmbH, Metzlerstrasse 26, 60594 Frankfurt am Main*

In Spain: Please write to *Penguin Books S. A., Bravo Murillo 19, 1° B, 28015 Madrid*

In Italy: Please write to *Penguin Italia s.r.l., Via Felice Casati 20, I–20124 Milano*

In France: Please write to *Penguin France S. A., 17 rue Lejeune, F–31000 Toulouse*

In Japan: Please write to *Penguin Books Japan, Ishikiribashi Building, 2–5–4, Suido, Bunkyo-ku, Tokyo 112*

In Greece: Please write to *Penguin Hellas Ltd, Dimocritou 3, GR–106 71 Athens*

In South Africa: Please write to *Longman Penguin Southern Africa (Pty) Ltd, Private Bag X08, Bertsham 2013*

BY THE SAME AUTHOR

Braided Lives

America in the fifties meant McCarthyism and Ban the Bomb,
jitterbug and jazz, girls in padded bras and clinging pastel twin-sets
– but that was not all . . .

In this story of the women who liberated us into the seventies, Marge
Piercy recreates the fear and tensions that lay beneath the surface.
Funny, angry and acidly entertaining, she writes of Jill, independent,
streetwise, and of her cousin and closest friend, Donna – braiding
lives before the Women's Movement, making love before the Pill.

'Impossible to put down . . . Marge Piercy just gets better and better
and better' – *Publisher's Weekly*

'Fine and funny . . . no writer I know of has so thoroughly explored
the world of a college girl becoming a woman' – *Washington Post*

'One of the most important novelists of our time' – Erica Jong

BY THE SAME AUTHOR

Vida

A dozen lovers, two hundred friends, thousands who had heard her speak at rallies . . .

In the sixties she was the symbol of passionate rebellion; now Vida Asch is forced to live as a fugitive. Years spent fleeing the FBI and travelling in disguise, and the experience of bitter sexual and political rivalries, threaten to splinter her commitment. In her struggle to survive Vida has learned to trust no one, but when another outcast, Joel, enters her circle, she finds herself reluctantly drawn to him . . .

In a novel that is fast-paced, often erotic and moving, Marge Piercy chronicles America's radical underground from the heady turmoil of the sixties to the disintegration of the seventies.

'Here is somebody with the guts to go into the deepest core of herself, her time, her history' – Thomas Pynchon

'A powerful novel, written with insight, wit and remorseless energy' – *The Times Literary Supplement*

BY THE SAME AUTHOR

Small Changes

In the sixties the world seemed to be making big changes – but for many women it was the small changes that were the hardest and the most profound.

On the surface Beth and Miriam were as different as two women could be. Shy and unsure of herself, Beth married her high-school sweetheart as soon as she had finished school. Aggressively intelligent and sensual, Miriam was determined to have an education and a career as well as a man. But both of them had been raised with images of how men and women were supposed to be. Both of them wanted love . . . expected it to fulfil them . . . expected it to last.

Small Changes – Marge Piercy's life-shattering novel about women and the choices they must face.

'We would have to look to a French writer like Colette or to American writers of another generation, like May Sarton, to find anyone who writes as tenderly as Marge Piercy about life's redeeming pleasures' – *Washington Book Review*

'One of the United States' key contemporary writers' – *City Limits*

BY THE SAME AUTHOR

Gone to Soldiers

The Winds of War, The Naked and the Dead, From Here to Eternity, The Young Lions – until now the passions, brutality and devastation of the Second World War have been written about only by men.

Marge Piercy's vast and involving novel follows the lives of ten men and women through their wartime experiences. Here, for the first time, one of America's major writers brings a woman's depth and intensity to the panorama of world war.

'A victory . . . Piercy fearlessly parachutes into male territory with powerful credibility and assurance' – *Newsweek*

'The reader is riveted to the page, eyes on stalks, stomach knotted, lump in the throat . . . a sense of elevation and new understanding follow' – *Observer*

'A book with a fat heart and full of real people, complex and contradictory . . . it's an important act of remembering, learning and healing' – *New Stateman*

'A huge novel in every sense of the word . . . may it flourish' – Margaret Atwood

BY THE SAME AUTHOR

Summer People

'Susan lives for the summer people. Now she wants to live like them.'

Every summer the noisy city people migrate to the pond on Cape Cod, disrupting the peace of its permanent, isolated community. Dinah grits her teeth until the woods are hers again and she is free to compose without their jarring discords. Willie shrugs and takes on their carpentry jobs to subsidize his real, winter life of sculpting. Only Susan, the pivotal member of their companionable *ménage à trois*, envies the glamour and excitement of these exotic visitors from another, wider world.

And when a series of chances brings the summer world closer to their own, Susan's envy swells to obsession – jolting the delicate balance of all their lives with a tragic crisis that threatens to shatter the harmony for ever . . .

'Her rendering of this triangular marriage is gritty, convinced, persuasive' – *Listener*

'Piercy writes with great tact about the dilemmas of her characters and their reactions to joy and tragedy. Perfect holiday reading . . . for long sunny afternoons accompanied by a glass or two of local wine' – *Evening Standard*

BY THE SAME AUTHOR

Body of Glass

'This is a tale of my family from long ago when the world seemed to be breaking open . . .'

In 1600 in a Jewish ghetto in Prague a 'golem' is brought to life to protect the inhabitants from attack by mobs that rise periodically to ravage and murder. In the 21st century the story continues . . .

In North America, scientist Shira Shipman joins forces with Yod, the world's most sophisticated cyborg, to guard her freetown, Tikva – a fragile modern ghetto in a land of rigidly controlled environmental corporate domes – from a gang of deadly intruders . . .

'A powerful, deeply felt parable about the individual versus the state' – *Cosmopolitan*

'*Body of Glass* is much more than science fiction. It's a touching love story (several, actually) and a gripping adventure tale . . . her best novel yet' – *St Louis Post Dispatch*

'Outstanding . . . I have not read a more disturbing or moving novel about an artificial intelligence since Mary Shelley's *Frankenstein* . . . it elevates its author to the pantheon of *haute* SF alongside Doris Lessing and Ursula Le Guin' – *Financial Times*

'A triumph of the imagination . . . a rich, complex tale so unique and so compelling it is simply impossible to put down' – Alice Hoffman

BY THE SAME AUTHOR

The Longings of Women

Mary Burke is homeless. Becky Burgess is awaiting trial for murder. Leila Landsman stands at a crossroads in her life. Three different women – each with a need to be loved, to be celebrated, to find a place in the world beyond the expectations of their families.

Mary cleans the houses of Boston's affluent families. At sixty-one, she remembers the time when she expected to grow old surrounded by comfort and love . . .

Becky struggles to leave her working-class roots behind her, only to find her ideals and ambitions dissolve into bleak routine and disillusion . . .

When her husband's latest affair goes one step too far, Leila realizes that her desires have yet to be discovered. Slowly, feeling the way, she begins to make changes . . .

'Every new novel by Marge Piercy is cause for celebration. *The Longings of Women* is a rich tapestry filled with passion and rage and real love, a book that gets under your skin and stays with you long after the last page has been turned' – Alice Hoffman

'I very much enjoyed Marge Piercy's *The Longing of Women*. It is full of her brand of tough compassion' – Marilyn French

'Stupendous . . . Piercy probes their dilemmas . . . with energy, humour and a steadfast and admirable lack of sentimentality' – *Sunday Telelgraph*